GOLF: *A Natural Course for Women*

GOLF:

Edited by James Lynch and Carole Collins

SANDRA HAYNIE

A Natural Course for Women

New York   1975   ATHENEUM

Copyright © 1975 by Sandra Haynie, James Lynch, and Carole Collins
All rights reserved
Library of Congress catalog card number 74-20359
ISBN 0-689-10650-5
Published simultaneously in Canada by McClelland and Stewart Ltd.
Manufactured in the United States of America by
The Book Press, Brattleboro, Vermont
Designed by Kathleen Carey
First Edition

To the five people who have meant the most to me
as a person and a professional

Foreword

SANDRA HAYNIE is the year's best woman golfer. In 1974 she won the United States Open and the Ladies Professional Golf Association of America titles in the same season—a feat matched only by one other player in the history of the LPGA, Mickey Wright. In addition, Sandra was tied for first in the other "big" tournament on the women's golf tour, the $200,000 Colgate–Dinah Shore Winners Circle, but lost the second hole of the play-off.

A model of consistency, Sandra won six of the eight tournaments she entered through September, including the $40,000 George Washington Classic, the $35,000 National Jewish Hospital Open, and the $40,000 Charity Golf Classic in Fort Worth. In earnings, she has passed the great Mickey Wright and now ranks second only to Kathy Whitworth.

Soon after picking up a golf club for the first time at the age

of eleven, Sandra Haynie was termed a "natural" golfer by some
of the top teaching pros in the country. She believes, though, that
every woman has the natural grace, timing and body control to
play an enjoyable game, if not a great game, and benefit from
doing so. This book is dedicated to that premise and to all those
women who have never known the exhiliration that can be found
on a golf course and need only to be shown how.

Contents

GOLF: *A Natural Course for Women*

Chapter ONE

Why Women Should Play Golf

BLUES, scarlets and purples colored the western sky as the setting sun shone through the moisture-laden air after a late afternoon storm. The painted sky formed a backdrop for the mountains and a lake and the long narrow stretch of emerald green grass where I stood on the top of a slight rise. What a sight, what a place to be, I thought, as the whole universe seemed to stand still with almost a hushed reverence. I wanted to shout or sing or do something wild, but then I looked down and saw that round, white dimpled sphere, a little more than an inch and a half in diameter, that was my world in professional golf.

Almost immediately, my concentration returned. I stole one last look at the beauty of the sky, sighted on the pin flag, hanging limply in the still air off to the side of the green, and started my backswing. Whack! The sound alone expressed everything I wanted to do or say when I first was entranced by the spectacular western sky. The ball soared far and true, and as I set off down the fairway, I thought again: What a place to be, what a wonderful life it is!

I don't know whether that was the start of my idea about writing a book, but certainly it was the epitome of my belief that golf is a natural course for women. There is no sport that I can think of that offers so much satisfaction, so much enjoyment and so many benefits to women as golf does. Not only are you able to get out in the fresh air away from the smog and air pollution of the cities (and the suburbs these days, too, unfortunately), but you also are able to enjoy nature. Of course, every day won't end with a beautiful sky and every drive won't be down the middle and close to the 200-yard mark, but it will still be rewarding fun.

I've been playing golf since I was eleven, but no woman is too old to take up the game and get genuine enjoyment out of it. You may never qualify for the Ladies Professional Golf Association of America tour, or even for your own club championship, but I think I can show you a way to play at your own level that will contribute to your physical and mental well-being. It doesn't matter if you are short or tall, thin or heavyset, or a combination. Whatever your contour may be, there is a natural way for you to play golf.

You may be a women who is already shooting in the 70s, or perhaps one who cards scores around 150—for 18 holes, not nine, please. Still others of you may never have held a golf club in your hand and have never set foot on a course. It really doesn't matter, golf is a game for all of you and there are different ways for each of you to accomplish your goals. For some of you, that will mean taking strokes off your score. For others, it might be merely a way to make yourself more interesting to your husband or boyfriend, to be in on the numerous golfing conversations and jokes that make the rounds whenever golfers get together. For still others, it might be the perfect answer to keeping your body toned up and attractive.

Aside from the appreciation of nature, the healthy exercise and the soothing effect that a round of golf can give you, there are other benefits. Golf has enough flexibility so that you can play in a threesome or a foursome or even play alone. Many clubs have husband-and-wife tourneys and mixed-foursome events where you can either get to know your husband better (and he may be a far different man in a bunker than at breakfast) or widen your circle of friends. You can go at your own speed, set your own goals and find satisfaction in overcoming the challenges inherent in each stroke, each hole, each course.

There is no better exercise in the world than walking, and that is at the heart of golf. Every round you play means a walk of at least three to five miles, depending on the length of the course—and how often you land in the rough or stray from the direct line of play. Naturally, there arc carts at most courses today, but I recommend that you walk the course, either pulling a bag cart or with a caddie carrying your clubs. If you feel you really need a cart, try walking between a few holes.

Walking the course before a tournament is vital to professionals so they can become familiar with the layout. No two golf courses are alike, and the strategy you figure out on a practice round before the competition starts frequently can mean the difference between a respectable showing and being far behind in the pack. For those of you just starting out on the game, though, walking can have other advantages. You can't listen to birds as well when you're riding in a golf cart, even though the noise level of the electric motors is extremely low; you can't watch the squirrels scampering through the rough as easily and you can't really fulfill the basic need for exercise.

When I said that golf could contribute to your mental well-being, I was not trying to take the place of your favorite shrink, although I hope that golf will enable you to dispense with such help, if you are getting it now. Certainly, you can take out your frustrations on those golf balls, and being out in the open away from the closed-in feeling that springs from our urban confinement and congestion is a glorious and intoxicating feeling.

Before I turned pro (and that was when I was only seventeen years old), I used to get up early every weekend morning and I could hardly wait to get out on the course. If I could just hit one or two balls that day the way I wanted to, I felt some kind of accomplishment—I had done something right. There is no way to describe the satisfaction of a coordinated swing until you go out there and do it yourself. Your whole body is in unison from the top of your swing all the way through. It's natural and it's right.

Some golfers I know—not on the pro tour, but just club golfers who enjoy the game even though they may never break 100—tell me about the satisfaction of getting off that good shot during a round that's almost a complete disaster. "That shot keeps me going," they say.

In this book I'd like to avoid being either too technical or too didactic, but rather to emphasize natural movements. I believe that women have the natural grace, style and ability to play golf easily and effortlessly. Naturally—there's that word again, and you'll see it throughout this book—you will play within your own capabilities. But whether you shoot in the 70s or in the 100s plus, you can still feel accomplishment and progress at your own level. You can play with those who are better than you to improve (some players insist that the better the competition, the better they play) or you can play with those at your own level for competition. You even might play with someone who has more to learn than you to give you the extra satisfaction of helping someone else.

What I want to do is give you some fundamentals about the game, the basics for a good golf swing and the ingredients that go into it: grip, stance and address. I use the word ingredients purposely, because it's just like a recipe: You may find a way that suits you better, just as you may find that two cups of sugar instead of a cup and a half is just right for your husband's favorite dessert. I don't want you to play like Sandra Haynie and I don't think you should try to play like Arnold Palmer. Do it your way, using the basics for a good golf swing: rhythm, timing and balance. Thus, as you see, there are six key factors—three before you even move the club and three when you are bringing it back and then hitting the ball. I'll explain them and then you try them, picking out the things I say that best apply to you.

Maybe you have the natural ability to sit down and read this book and then go out and shoot in the 70s. If you do, fine, there's a spot on the golf tour for you. Perhaps you're the type of person who will never break 100, but still you can get as much fun, relaxation and physical and mental benefits as the 70 shooter. In either case, I'd like to make it clear that a good instructor is a must. This book is not intended to take the place of a good golf instructor. I hope to give you some fundamentals. The swing itself is such an individual thing that you'll need the analysis of a golf pro to tell you what you are doing right and wrong. Practice your swing until you feel comfortable and natural.

No two people are built exactly alike. Some people are long-legged and others have short legs with a long trunk. It's the same way with feet; the shoe size may be the same, but each person has a distinctive walk, a way of putting her feet down that sets her off as an individual.

Warren Cantrell, the first golf teacher I had, used to say that he could tell whether a person is a golfer by the way he or she

walks toward him. There are other people who say that they can
tell policemen, ex-fighters, wrestlers, mailmen, etc., by the way
they walk, but I'm not one of them. I say regardless of how you
walk, you can learn to play golf naturally and easily without ac-
cepting dogma or following rules that will make you uncomfort-
able or self-conscious.

Besides being the director of golf for the city of Lubbock,
Texas, Warren Cantrell is a professional engineer and builder.
Perhaps his training as an engineer gives him an insight into planes
of motion and stresses that escapes other people, but at any rate
I guess that I owe my start in golf to him.

One day, when I was eleven years old, I accompanied my
father to the golf course. Dad was a very good amateur player and
he was getting some instructions from Warren on the practice tee
when I walked up to see what was going on.

"Do you know that girl?" Warren asked my father. Later he
said that my walk had fulfilled all the requirements of a potential
golfer—balance, ease and natural grace.

"That's my daughter, Sandra Jane," Dad said. "Sandy, come
over here and say hello to Mr. Cantrell."

"Do you mind if she hits a few balls for me?" Warren asked,
interested, I guess, in testing his theory.

"Not at all, go right ahead," Dad said. "I'll meet you back in
the clubhouse." I guess he didn't want to be embarrassed, but at
any rate he left.

Warren gave me an old No. 6 iron and 30 practice balls. I had
watched Dad and the other golfers around the course quite a bit,
so I just did what was natural for me, I hit the balls, and Warren's
eyes seemed to become bigger as I went through the whole lot
without a miss. Usually, I found out later, even good golfers muff
a shot or two when they are practicing. That convinced Warren

that his instant analysis was right and he spent 45 minutes with me before rejoining Dad in the clubhouse. He left me on the practice tee and I continued to hit with that old No. 6 iron. Even today, the iron game is my strong point and I often wonder if that groove wasn't established the first time I picked up a club.

Finding your own groove is what golf is all about. Ben Hogan, a fellow Texan, has written a golf book, Arnold Palmer has written a golf book, and a lot of the other top men professionals have done the same. The problem as I see it is they each say, "This is how I do it, you should do the same." First of all, not everyone is as small and wiry as Bantam Ben and not everyone has the strength of Palmer. The tone of the books seem to be that the Hogan method or the Palmer method must work for everyone, man or woman. I find this hard to accept.

First of all, golf instructional books by men do not apply to women. In this society, the male is caught up in competition either in his job or in sports. The accent on winning means that there is a narrow mentality that can be translated only into victory to be meaningful. Another point is that what will work well for Ben Hogan or Arnold Palmer might not for John Smith or Mrs. Smith —particularly the latter. That's why I stress doing your own thing.

Too much technical knowledge can be harmful in golf, I believe. You don't have to know why a particular shot is working well for you just so it does work and you can do it over and over again. Too often people will stuff their heads full of technical knowledge and go out on the course and find that they don't know how to apply the techniques to their own physical make-up or their abilities. Worse than that, they can be so full of dogma—keep your left arm straight, keep your head still, etc.—that instead of relaxing and doing what is natural and enjoying themselves, they put themselves through an ordeal.

Interpretations are important, of course. For instance, when a book says keep your left arm straight, it might be assumed that the left arm should be straight all through the golf swing. Now that's just plain abnormal. You can't keep your left arm straight throughout and have a correct, natural swing. The left arm has to bend at the top of your backswing and at the end of your follow-through. And what about the left-handers?

I remember one time in Fort Worth at a press conference. After all the questions were finished, a woman came over to me. She was almost in tears.

"You just have to talk to my husband," she said.

That was a puzzler because I had never seen the woman before, but fortunately people find it fairly easy to communicate with me. I learned in the subsequent conversation that the woman, who was then forty-five years old, wanted to take up golf, but she had played tennis and baseball as a left-hander, and now her husband was insisting that he wouldn't buy her left-handed golf clubs. If she was going to learn to play, he said, she'd have to do it as a right-hander, which is the way most of the books are written—for right-handers.

I did speak to her husband and told him that he was frustrating every natural instinct the woman had toward sports. I said that he would be putting a tremendous handicap on the woman both physically and mentally if he insisted on trying to convert her to a right-hander. I wasn't sure that I had convinced him, but I saw the woman several months later and she was effusive in her thanks. She had her left-handed clubs and she was having a ball learning to play the game her own way. Score one more for the natural way.

This woman, of course, took up golf quite late in life, but she enjoyed it nevertheless. Most of the women on the pro tour started around the same age I did, or shortly thereafter. Of course, like any profession we have our child prodigies, too. Marlene Hagge, for instance, started playing golf when she was three and a half. That was because her father was a golf pro, and while other fathers might play other games with their daughters, Dave thought Marlene would enjoy golf; she certainly has for a good number of years. Other earlier starters among the pros were Kathy Ahern, who began shooting for pars to please pa when she was five, and Cathy Walker, a comparative newcomer, who took up the game when she was eight.

One of the problems about starting the game young, particularly if you do not have proper instruction, as all of the women on the tour have had, is that you might pick up bad habits which will be hard to break. Because you picked up your own style of swinging, you may have developed a hitch that a purist would say must be eliminated.

Everything is going along smoothly until one day someone says, "You have an awful hitch in your golf swing, you should try to get rid of it." Why? If you've been playing with the hitch—a jerky, or awkward movement—for all the years since you took up the game, forget it. If you try to lose the hitch, you could be getting yourself into the position where you'd never be able to hit the ball. If the hitch is part of the total pattern of your golf swing, you're doing what is natural for you. I'm not saying that you can't improve your game, even if you do have a hitch in your swing. Through some simple and understanding instructions you can improve on your timing and smooth out your rhythm. Timing and rhythm help to create accuracy and distance on the golf course, off the tees and on the fairways.

Don't get me wrong. If a woman professional has a hitch in her swing or she should suddenly develop one, she's going to work on it steadily because she feels it can hurt her game. That's her job—scoring better and getting into the money, and you can be sure that everyone wants to improve at her job. The big difference is that the professional has the time to spend on the practice tees that the amateur does not.

I guess that's how my father and Warren Cantrell came to realize that I was destined to become a golf professional—because I was willing to make the sacrifices to improve. You remember my first encounter with that old No. 6 iron? After I had hit the balls to Warren's satisfaction, he went to the clubhouse and I stayed out on the practice tee whaling away at the balls. The click of the contact with the metal and the cover of the ball and the soaring arc of the flights of the balls gave me a thrill. After about 45 minutes, I went in to see Warren to ask him a question. I think it was something about my grip, although I could be wrong. At any rate, I got the answer and went back to the tee to apply what Warren had told me.

"You know, Jim," Warren said to my father as I walked away, "only about four or five golfers ever asked me that question." I certainly wish I could remember what it was. Be that as it may, the answer must have been even more intriguing and the results I obtained even better and more satisfying than the original 45-minute session. I kept at it for more than three hours and when I quit my hands were swollen. I was pleased, because I had impressed my father, and what eleven-year-old doesn't want to do that?

After that I started playing golf, but I wasn't sure how serious I was about the game. My father was doing all that he could to encourage me because there is a great tradition of golf in Texas. Babe Zaharias, one of the all-time greats, was just starting to make headlines as a golfer when I was four years old. Babe was one of the founders of the Ladies Professional Golf Association and she was a great lady, with dignity, skill and courage, as everyone familiar with her story knows. I don't know whether Dad envisioned me as another Babe Zaharias, or another Patty Berg, who was just about at the top of her game then, but he did have something in mind because he was always cautioning me to be careful or not to engage in certain activities since I might hurt muscles that were essential in golf.

Perhaps those parental restrictions were responsible for the uncertainty in my mind about what I'd like to become. I was playing golf for about 11 months or so when I met the man who shaped my game and made a lasting impression on my character. That man was A. G. Mitchell, a lovely Scotsman who was seventy-two years old when I first met him at the Rivercrest Country Club, where I had gone to play in a tournament.

The Scots are a fine people, warm and friendly and helpful. As you know, golf was invented in Scotland and as a result many of the people from that country regard the game with a kind of reverence. A. G. Mitchell—Mr. Mitch as I always called him—was one of those men who thought that golf was the perfect game and that those who could play it well had a divine gift. He was retired when I met him that day at Rivercrest, but he used to go out to the club a couple of days a week just to keep in touch with the game. I don't know whether it was my walk, which Warren Cantrell had noticed, but at any rate Mr. Mitch was attracted to me and we got to talking. He had taught some of the great golfers who came out of Texas, including Babe Zaharias, so I was properly in awe of him.

Mr. Mitch, though, was a wonderful human being as well as a great teacher and he soon put me at ease. I told him that I wasn't sure if I wanted to make golf my life. He offered to be my instructor and I was flattered, but my father was really thrilled. I was an only child, and there were always two counter forces working on me during my early life: My mother wanted me to stay home and let her do everything for me and my father wanted me to get out in the world and be someone. That chance meeting with Mr. Mitch changed my life. He not only taught me the basics of my golf game as I play today, but he also gave me a philosophy that drew parallels between life and golf. In both you can always know the direction you want to go in, you can always know how you are going to get there and you can think about it before you set out.

After a year of Mr. Mitch's instructions, I knew that golf would be my life. By the time I was thirteen, I was taking off from school in the spring to get out to the course as much as possible. Mr. Mitch built my game along the lines I've mentioned earlier—the natural way.

If you're going to be tolerant of mistakes, he'd say, then you're going to have habits—in other words, the same mistakes would occur over and over again. If I have problems, the precepts that Mr. Mitch gave me enable me to narrow my troubles down to a few basic areas. One of the most important things he taught me, though, was humility. He couldn't abide conceited athletes and he had his own subtle way of getting you to keep your feet on the ground. I remember when I started winning tournaments, he used to say: "Is your hat still the same size?" Of course, I was just glowing because I was pleased with myself and pleased that my father was proud of me, but I don't think I was ever conceited. I just considered it lucky that I had won—that's a paraphrase, I guess, of Mr. Mitch's idea about being blessed with talent—but I've always said I'd rather be lucky than good. Come to think of it, there was a baseball player, Lefty Gomez of the Yankees, who used to say the same thing.

At any rate, my luck started to click when I won the Texas Public Links championship in June of 1957. I had just turned fourteen the week of the tournament, and when I received that trophy I was certain that nothing was so rare as a day in June, with my picture in the papers, my father smiling in the background and all that fuss over just doing what came naturally and having fun. The next year I won the title again and also went on to a little faster company, winning the Texas State Amateur. In the Lone Star State, that was the big apple for women, because all of the members of the country clubs, those who were out there every day of the week working on their game, were in the competition. In the Public Links tournament, you are more apt to run up against the weekend golfer or the occasional player. At any rate, I won the Texas Amateur in 1958 and repeated in 1959, and at the ripe old age of sixteen I was looking for new worlds to conquer.

Mr. Mitch, of course, was delighted. He used to say that I was the light of his old age. He also used another expression that was reported to me second-hand, but it meant an awful lot to me when you consider some of the great golfers that Mr. Mitch had taught. "All of my girls had something, but my baby has it all." Of course, I was "his baby" and the compliment meant more to me than some of the trophies and tournaments I've won.

Unfortunately, Mr. Mitch's happiness about my progress in golf was blighted by some bad news from his doctor. He had leukemia. He told me about it because, I guess, he wanted me to start thinking about another instructor. "I have about three years to live," he said with the simple dignity that marked all his words. I wanted to cry or run away or do something to shut the thought out of my mind, but Mr. Mitch hadn't taught me that way and he wasn't that way himself. I resolved that I would spend every minute I could with him and absorb as much of his philosophy and personality and knowledge as possible. I suppose it was selfish, but I'd like to think that I am repeating some of it in this book.

We were living in Austin at the time I learned of Mr. Mitch's illness, and Austin is about three and a half hours away from Fort Worth, even the way Texans drive. I was constantly bugging my father to drive me into Fort Worth so I could see Mr. Mitch. Dad was sympathetic, but it was a long drive and I wasn't old enough to drive myself. Fortunately, my mother's folks lived in Fort Worth so there were some excuses—Dad could always take mother to see her family or visit his in-laws while I was out at Rivercrest with Mr. Mitch.

Mr. Mitch's ambition was that I would gain a place on the Curtis Cup golf team, which represents the United States in matches against women from Britain. I guess he thought that if one of his pupils took his precepts back to the old country it would be his tribute to the royal and ancient game. I'm afraid I disappointed him. When I did qualify, I had reached a crossroads in my life and decided to follow the path toward the professional ranks, which would eliminate me from consideration as a Curtis Cupper.

The turning point came in the spring of 1960 when I was playing in the Trans-Mississippi tournament, one of the biggest amateur events in the country. The champions of most of the Southern states were there and so were some top-notch golfers from all over the country. Rather than being awed, I was perfectly at ease and managed to win the tournament, getting one of the biggest trophies I had seen. Then I began to think: Did I want to collect silverware that had to be polished and dusted or did I want to match my game against the professionals, the top golfers in the country? The LPGA was about ten years old at the time and although the purses were nowhere near what they are today, a lot of the women were making respectable livings doing what I enjoyed so much. Besides, amateur golf could be expensive. Dad never complained, but I knew that he was sometimes strapped to get the travel money for tournaments.

When you're an amateur, you get nothing back for the major outlay that the big tournaments necessitate. Also, you can only play in one or two big tournaments each summer, as the rest of the time you're playing on a citywide or a statewide level and your competition is limited. If I stayed an amateur, the next logical step was college and I dreaded the thought of that.

I have nothing against college educations. In fact, we have a lot of highly educated women on the pro tour and they weren't all physical education majors either. We have doctors and nurses and even one golfer who has a Ph.D. in physics. For me, though, high school was enough, possibly because it was taking me away from my true love—golf.

It wasn't an easy decision. There were family conferences and long talks with Mr. Mitch. My family was willing to accept my point of view, but Mr. Mitch was deeply hurt. If I turned pro, that meant that his dream for me, playing on the Curtis Cup team, would not be possible. To Mr. Mitch, I guess, I had plenty of time and he had so little. Still, I was determined and I got some encouragement from one source—George Alexander. George was the pro at Rivercrest when I first met Mr. Mitch so he had been acquainted with me and my game for some time. He was a good friend and a good instructor—in fact, after the death of Mr. Mitch, George became my principal teacher and I would fly back to Fort Worth whenever I was getting into trouble with some aspect of my game. George also is the instructor for Kathy Ahern and Kathy Farrer, two other members of the pro tour, as well as scores of top-grade amateurs.

At any rate, George was the one positive force in supporting my decision to turn pro. He knew what was on my mind and he thought that I had the strokes to match with the best. At least he knew that I would never really be happy until I faced that chal-

lenge. Mr. Mitch took it hard. He didn't abandon me, of course—
he wasn't that kind of a man—he swallowed his disappointment, or
at least tried to. I always like to think that had he lived to see what
I've accomplished as a professional, he would have been proud of
me. Unfortunately, he passed away when I had been a pro only
two years and not too many laurels came my way in that period.

In that first year, I played in 12 tournaments and my best
finish was a tenth in the San Antonio Open. Oddly enough, Carol
Mann, the girl who had led the qualifying round in the Trans-
Mississippi tournament that I won, turned pro the same year and
she finished eleventh in the San Antonio Open. As two of the
rookies on the tour, Carol and I became friends, and that friend-
ship has endured through the years. I'm proud to serve as vice
president under her in the LPGA. At 6 feet 3 inches, Carol is the
tallest woman on the tour and she towers over my 5 feet 5 inches.
Like me, she is a blue-eyed blonde, and she has a great sense of
humor.

A lot of people didn't think that Carol's game had quite the
polish it should have had when she came on the pro tour, but she
is a hard worker. She worked on her game for two solid years on
the tour without a victory. She was a good amateur player, the
experts said, but she didn't have the solid game that would stand
up under the constant pressure of playing every day for 35 weeks
of the year. However, she found a good instructor, one she could
communicate with, and she set about to rebuild her golf swing
completely. It took guts to do that while playing on the tour, but
that's the kind of person Carol is.

In contrast, I don't feel that I work hard at my game, possibly
because of my philosophy of doing things naturally. Golf just
seems to come natural to me, which probably is that luck I spoke
about. I think I'd have to mention Pat Stapler in that connection

because she was an influence on my approach to the game. We were living in Midland, Texas, at the time I started to play and Pat was one of the top players in the area. She was easygoing and soft-spoken and her golf swing was just a pattern of beautiful rhythm. There is something about soft, gentle people that isn't always discernible—a quiet aggressiveness that gets the job done when more pushy types are likely to fall flat on their faces. Pat Stapler was that kind of a person and so is Mickey Wright.

Mickey is the kind of a woman who knows what she can do and does it. She doesn't brag about what she's going to do, she just goes out and performs. That's how she got to be a member of the LPGA Hall of Fame. The year I started on the pro tour, Mickey won ten of the 17 events she competed in, including her second-straight LPGA title.

I don't know if Pat Stapler could have done as well, because Pat never went on the pro tour. She turned pro so she could take on paying students, because she was divorced and needed income to support her two children. I've always felt that Pat could have been right up there with the great ones if she could have taken that beautiful swing out in top competition.

I remember receiving congratulations from Pat on my first pro victory. I think she was in the gallery for most of the tournament, but I can't be sure because I was so intense that I hardly knew what was going on around me. No time to appreciate beautiful sunsets then; it was at the Austin Civitan Open, which marked the first and only pro tournament held in Austin, and for me it was sort of a homecoming. I had lived in Austin, grown up there and done most of my playing out of Austin, so I was certainly one of the gallery's favorites. To a lot of people I was Jim Haynie's Sandy trying to look all grown up at the age of eighteen by competing with the best golfers in the country.

There was more than one cry of "Go get 'em, Sandy," or "Good shot, Sandy," as I made my way around the course. Dad, of course, was there and I felt some pressure because I didn't want to let him down in front of all his friends. There was no worry about that, though; I finished with a 7-under-par 289 and for the first time in my life I received a check along with the winner's trophy. I thought I was on my way at long last and the next week when I won the Cosmopolitan Open, I was sure.

Chapter _TWO_

Exercises to Get You Ready

Sᴏᴍᴇ women have an inferiority complex about playing golf —or any sport, for that matter—particularly when they take it up late in life. They're afraid that they'll be making a spectacle of themselves and they feel awkward. Fortunately, this feeling is dying down because of the new emphasis on doing your own thing. I do think, though, that any woman taking up golf or going back to it after a long layoff would be wise to do some simple exercises. Otherwise, when she gets on the course she is going to rediscover some long-unused muscles, and the resultant discomfort might turn her off the game.

There are probably as many different theories about physical conditioning as there are religions—in fact, conditioning and fitness have become a virtual religion with some people. What I intend to do is let you be the judge of what is best for you. I'll give you the guidelines and you pick out what fills your needs and suits your temperament. Here again the matter of goals comes into the picture. Certainly the legs are important to golf, but you don't have to jog or ride a bicycle so hard that you develop grotesque leg muscles. From what I've heard from the girl-watchers in the gallery, there are a lot of shapely legs on the pro tour—you don't need "piano legs" to play good golf.

The same applies to your back and shoulder muscles. You can build them up with barbells or the like, but the primary thing you should aim for is flexibility. A good exercise for this is to hold a golf club behind your neck and bend and twist. It's something like you see the baseball players do when they're going up to bat. You want those muscles to stretch and be supple, but they need not be overdeveloped.

The forearms, the wrists and the hands are the parts of the body that should be strengthened if you want to play good golf. The fortunate part about this is that you can have tremendous strength in your wrists and hands and yet be eminently qualified to pose for a glove commercial or one of those ads for hand cream. Primarily what you are strengthening are tendons and getting them used to strains that are exerted throughout the golf swing and especially at the instant of impact. Theoretically, if a woman can lift a bag of groceries in the supermarket or lift a baby from a crib, she is getting exercise for her forearms, wrists and hands. However, there are special tricks that will help when you start off on the first tee.

For instance, take a dry towel, hold it taut and just wring it back and forth. This is excellent exercise for the wrists, as is any turning maneuver. You can pick up a telephone book and hold it at arms length and just turn it slowly. This is also good for the back muscles because they are extended as you reach out. The one thing I want to stress, though, is easy does it. Don't knock yourself out the first day or the first session. If you get physically tired easily, do about ten wrings of the towel or ten turns of the phone book and then quit. Go back to do ten more in an hour or two or even three. Meanwhile, you can be sweeping the floor—which is exercise, too—and thinking of golf. There's an analogy there, you know. The broom is the equivalent of your club, the floor is the fairway, the dust is the ball and the dustpan is the green. The idea is to move the dust over the fairway and onto the green with a smooth sweep, just as the idea is to move the ball onto the green with a smooth stroke. That sort of exercise is called conditioning. I believe it helps to think positively, but again, it's all up to you.

There are some difficult things about golf for women to master, but really it's merely mind over matter. Some women feel that they are taking a foreign object—the club—and timing their body movements to hit this small object, which is sitting still. How about a fly buzzing around your kitchen? You'd have no trouble getting out the fly swatter and letting the fly have it, would you? It's basically the same thing.

Because I started playing golf early, I was in shape virtually every time I picked up a club. At first, I was also doing a lot of swimming and serving as a lifeguard to buy the things that typical teenagers want. Swimming, like golf, is a terrific muscle toner.

You will burn up calories playing golf, but essentially it is not a punishing sport where you can expect to take off weight. You can make it that way if you want, but that takes all the fun out of the game.

Take Donna Caponi Young, for example. Donna, who won the United States Open title in 1969 and 1970, started playing golf when she was eight years old because her father was a pro in California. In high school, she won seven varsity letters and on the golf tour she was so crazy about music and dancing that she was called Watusi. Well, everyone says that dancing is great exercise, especially some of the more energetic ones, but Donna never seemed to lose a pound. She wasn't fat, but she was solid despite all the calories she was burning up on the dance floor and the golf course. Through a special diet she lost 35 pounds in 1972, which proves that exercise alone will not take off the pounds. You'll merely be converting blubber to muscle in many cases, and you'll need the discipline of the diet if you are really to overcome a weight problem.

The beauty of golf is that the big and the short and the tall and the fat and the thin and the solid can compete, with proper muscle toning. If you're big-busted, you might have to develop a swing that will make you move the upper part of your body differently from a flat-chested woman. You'll be swinging around your bust, in effect, but you won't be losing anything because you'll be doing what is natural for you.

Because of the stress on physical fitness—Marilyn Smith, a three-time president of the LPGA, is on the President's Council for Physical Fitness—I think that the women coming on the tour as rookies these days are better physical specimens. Also, when I turned pro, I was barely 5 feet 2 inches and weighed only 105 pounds; extra inches and pounds have added leverage and momentum to my swing, so even though it might not have changed basically, it has picked up power and distance. Many of the girls are more mature, because they are coming on the tour not after high school, but after college, like JoAnn Washam, my roommate on the tour since 1973. JoAnn is a graduate of Washington State, and although she still hasn't broken into the winner's circle, she has all the equipment and all the dedication she needs. She's getting help from a lot of players on the tour, including Kathy Whitworth and me, and you'll probably be seeing her name in the papers a lot in the next few years.

Neither JoAnn nor I smoke or drink, which must be brought up in any discussion about conditioning. I don't want to get preachy, but you'll find that your stamina is a lot better, you'll get tired less easily and you'll enjoy the round more if you don't smoke. There are all sorts of statistics to back up my assertion, but if you're addicted to the weed no one is going to change you except yourself.

I prefer a soft drink to alcohol. In fact, I'll frequently have a Coke in the morning instead of coffee—that's my bag. One thing about a soda bottle, you can grasp it firmly and then relax the pressure a couple of times so that you're getting exercise for your fingers. Another way might be to squeeze one of your children's toys, or a small rubber ball. Some people say that playing a guitar or playing the piano or even typing are good finger exercise, but you can't convince me. I think I have pretty strong fingers and wrists, but I can't play the guitar for long without getting tired. It's the same way with the piano. I can play, but I get tired quickly. Maybe the movements are different and the golf grip requires less suppleness than playing piano. Of course, my rhythm, my music, comes out on the course, with the soft breezes blowing, the solid click of the club against the ball, and then that most satisfying of all final notes when the ball drops into the cup.

This isn't to say that you should give up the piano if you want to play golf. I'm sure some fine pianists make great golfers. We have some girls on the tour who can fill in for the professional players at club when there's dancing, but it's an individual thing, which is my sum total approach to golf, conditioning and life itself. No one can tell you what to do. I can tell you that this works, that works and so does something else. Just as in life, you are presented with options; it's up to you to decide which suit you best.

There is a whole cult that says dancing—belly dancing, no less—is a great physical conditioner for women. I don't quarrel with that thesis at all, but I just don't see myself in a veil prancing around with a diamond in my navel to get ready for a big tournament. Similarly, yoga has its advocates, and there are those who swear that the lotus position is not only the solution to all their physical problems but also to all the world's problems.

I would have trouble assuming the lotus position because of a knee operation I had a couple of years ago. I should have had the operation sooner, but I was stubborn, which is a trait that seems to be associated with people from Texas. I was injured in 1966 when I fell off a curb—a stupid thing to do, I know, but that's how it happened. It didn't stop me from playing golf, though. I was out on the tour for nine months a year and then during the off season I'd use crutches to give the knee rest so that it would heal properly. Of course, it never did and then finally the doctors told me that my knee would probably lock on me and require surgery. I quit the tour in August and went home to my parents. The surgery was performed in Fort Worth and I didn't join the tour until the next season, in January.

Mentally, I was ready to get back to work, but my leg wasn't really completely healed. Still I felt that Mr. Mitch's training to compensate for mistakes could be utilized to compensate for the stiffness in my leg. It was a year before I got back into shape again, but I've always liked challenges on the golf course and playing against the top players when I was not in the pink of condition gave me a drive and an incentive that made that year one of the most rewarding and satisfying of my career.

So many adhesions had built up in my knee during the long delay in having the operation that I had to go back into the hospital to have the adhesions broken—since they were not breaking down naturally. I was in the hospital two weeks before I was scheduled to tee off in Miami. When I got out of the hospital I was on crutches for four or five more days and then I hobbled around for an additional four or five days before I hit a couple of balls. I went down to Miami with virtually no practice and with a stiff leg, but still tied for first and lost only in the playoff.

Karate, jujitsu and kung fu all have their adherents as great body conditioners. Certainly they will give you some protection against overardent country club swains or unsavory characters you might meet on some of the streets of cities these nights, but I'm not too sure if they are applicable to the preparation for golf. If you find that they are, fine. Another type of exercise that appeals to me, because I consider myself lazy, is the stretching exercises. Following this method, the movements of the cat are emulated, slowly and sensuously stretching the muscles in your arms, back, neck and legs. Women have always been regarded as sort of feline creatures and these stretching movements can turn nervous fatigue into a pleasant feeling of physical relaxation.

I stumbled on this plan during a tournament in Portland, Oregon. I had been up until one o'clock in the morning discussing some problems of the LPGA with the other officers and I had a relatively early tee-off time the next morning. Before I got out of bed, I sort of stretched and then relaxed a minute before getting dressed. I had been mentally and physically tired the night before and therefore didn't get much sleep, but I was able to go out and play a fairly good round, although I can't remember what I shot. Of course, discipline enters into such a regimen; if you have the discipline, you can relax and concentrate.

Stretching ties in well with golf because both tend to tone your muscles. The tension that many people feel between their shoulder blades can be eased by a series of stretching exercises. You might not need that back massage or that neck massage you get from your husband if you do get into the stretching routine, but if you like it, by no means give it up. Massage and stretching could go well together.

Stretching can be done in bed, against a wall, in a doorway or even on the tee while you are waiting for your partner or your rival to drive. In bed, the best way is to lie on your back, with your arms out at shoulder level and with your palms up. The back of your wrists should be firmly down on the mattress. Bend your knees and raise them as high as you can toward your chest. In this position, roll your knees from one side to the other, trying not to rest them on the mattress, but holding them just a fraction away from that support.

Against a wall, stand sideways at arms' length from the wall with your feet together. Brace one arm against the wall, making sure the elbow is straight. If you start with your left arm against the wall, extend your left leg toward the wall, shifting your weight to your right foot. Now raise your right arm over your head, with the palm facing away from the wall and stretch your body to form the letter C. If you stretch your arm, you'll feel the stretch from your wrist to your hips. Repeat with the right hand against the wall. This is especially good for loosening up the hips, which are very important in golf.

A good stretching exercise for the neck muscles and the waist can be done in a standing position, with your hands clasped low behind your back. With your weight on your right leg, extend your left leg to the side and then pull down on your left arm and turn your head to the left so you can see your left heel. Your left shoulder will dip down as you pull on your arm and you'll feel the delightful stretching of the neck muscles. As I understand it, stretching gets the lactic acids out of the muscles, and since these acids are what cause us to feel tired, their removal gives us a new feeling of freshness.

The doorway exercise is a simple one, too. All you have to do is reach as high as you can and press outward against the frame. With your head held high and your elbows straight, contract your abdominal muscles and lean forward with your chest. You'll be surprised at the kinks this will take out of your spine, your neck and your shoulders.

No discussion of physical fitness for women would be complete, I guess, without touching on the female chemistry as manifested by our monthly periods. This can be more of a problem on the pro tour than for the amateur player, but it is a factor for her too. There are certain times of the month when your hands get so puffy you can hardly get them around a golf club. The three or four changes our bodies go through each month leave us a bit emotional and this can upset timing. Still, I feel that these are things you have to play with; even if your timing is off, you can still get around the course and enjoy it. And, they say, walking is the best exercise for menstrual cramps. Of course, some women have more trouble than others and on the tour some have such severe cramps that they take medication to get them through a round. This will make them either slow and drowsy or fast and hyperactive—no cause for a saliva test, though, since it won't make that much difference in scoring.

Since physical exercise releases tension, you can take your frustrations out on that little white pill—the golf ball, I mean, not THE Pill. The ball furnishes an outlet for your aggression; it's like a punching bag. But it has to be hit skillfully. And yet, while you are using the game as a physical outlet, if you have developed the timing, balance and rhythm that I've mentioned so much, you're going to be playing well and enjoying yourself. Don't try to kill the ball, though, in working off your frustrations. Be natural, take it easy.

Don't ever think that you are going to overpower the ball the way many men do. Men are simply stronger, in the legs, in the hips, in the shoulders and in the wrists. They can make mistakes, but the strength and the aggressiveness with which they attack a golf course will frequently bail them out. A lot of women play that way, too, but that happens to be their nature. I consider myself aggressive, but I play the course with caution. I play conservatively, trying not to waste strokes.

A lot of men come up to me and say, "You're so little and I weigh 230 pounds and you can drive that ball farther than I can. What's up?" Mind you, this is an amateur golfer talking, not one of the men pros. Essentially, the answer is what I've been saying all along. Mickey Wright says it this way: "The only way for a woman to compensate for her relative lack of physical strength is for her to build an efficient, repeating golf swing, utilizing a square club-face position throughout the golf swing with good balance and rhythm." Sal Di Buono, the veteran pro at the Bonnie Briar Country Club in Larchmont, New York, says: "Women learn to generate club-head speed with the hands and timing, not brute strength. They don't try to overpower the ball or muscle it the way strong men do."

Actually, I think that the average male amateur can learn from watching the women professionals. When they watch the men pros, who have all that brute strength, they get the feeling that they, too, have to overpower the ball with every shot. If they watch the women, though, they'll pick up hints about timing, rhythm and balance. They'll ease up on their swings and they'll probably find that they are doing a lot better, hitting the ball straighter and knocking strokes off their scores. It's just a question of ego: whether a man will admit that he learned something by watching a woman. Personally, I'd just as soon eliminate all the references and comparisons between men and women and just regard everyone as a human being.

If you have noticed, no one has ever said that anything except rhythm, balance and timing go into a good golf swing. The strength is a plus and is one reason why the men's tees and the women's tees are different distances. On most golf courses there are three sets of tees, although some have as many as five sets of tees with a children's course and a par-3 layout integrated into the regular course. This usually is at recreational communities, which have sprung up in amazing numbers in various parts of the country. It's heartening to me that most of these recreational communities are built around a golf course, with the idea that the whole family can take up the game. I think this could lead to a whole new breed of golfers in the coming generation because the potential of all the states will be tapped instead of the warm-weather states, where golf is now so firmly established.

The three basic tees, though, are the men's tees, the women's tees and the championship tees. The championship tees can be as much as 20 to 50 yards behind the men's tees, which makes the game longer and more challenging. Usually, these markers are used only for tournaments. The women's tees are 20 to 50 yards in front of the men's tees, shortening the course for women and making the game, in theory at least, easier. In some instances, women's par will be less than men's par and in some instances it will be higher. It depends on the layout of the course. Usually, during the tournament tour, the women professionals play from the men's tees. Since we are handicapped at the start by our inability to match the men in driving power, we usually get a break on the longer holes by having the par higher than men's par.

On the average golf course, I don't think that the women's tees are far enough ahead of the men's tees. If I'm playing against a man who can outdrive me by 50 yards, I should tee off 50 yards ahead of where he is setting up his ball; that's the only way to equalize things. I don't enjoy using the men's tees; they are just too long. They take some of the enjoyment out of the game for me because I don't want to be using woods all the time. I want to hit maybe one or two woods, but I also want to be able to hit some long iron shots and I want to hit a lot of short irons. When I go with the driver, then the No. 2 or No. 3 wood for two shots more, I'm not having a good time, I'm just having a long day.

Perhaps this feeling comes through because I'm good with irons and I think that most women have a better touch with their irons than with their woods. Betsy Rawls, for instance, a member of the LPGA Hall of Fame and a four-time winner of the U.S. Open and holder of two LPGA titles, has never been known as a strong driver. Yet her shotmaking is considered among the best in the game, as her record of 55 victories shows. She has twice been ranked as an All-American for trouble shots in the *Golf Magazine* players' poll, and once said that she "could get the ball down in two out of a tin can."

About the only time the women professionals get to play with men is in the pro-amateur events that are part of the preliminaries to big tournaments. I've played with Don Adams, the comedian, Robert Goulet, the singer, and Joe Namath, the Jets' quarterback. At first I thought that they'd be playing to the gallery, but I found each of them fine gentlemen and a real joy to play with. Don Adams was terrific. According to him, I was the most important thing happening that day, everything he did was secondary. He was such a big help; he said he just wanted to stay out of my way.

I was really surprised by Robert Goulet. He's so handsome and seems to dominate the stage when he's on it that I really didn't know what to expect. As it was, he couldn't have been nicer. It's almost as if he realized that in essence I was the star and he was the supporting player. A lot of times you expect the celebrities to be kind of impressed with themselves and try to turn the crowd on to them. Bob Hope, I know, jokes a lot, but he is also a good golfer and can help his side when a stroke or two is needed.

Most celebrities know that you are out there playing for money and it's not a light thing or a frivolous thing with you. As a result, you are their No. 1 concern. They don't want to do anything to embarrass you or hurt your chances of getting into the money. It's very nice to feel kind of protected by them.

Joe Namath really has that rare quality that's called charisma. I think the world of Joe. He's a very talented man and he's just as nice as he is talented. One thing that impressed me about Joe was that every time we came off a tee or a green, the little boys would just mob him for his autograph. He never refused them, but he made sure that he moved them over and got them out of my path where I could get to the tee without any interruptions and just go about my business. It was a small thing on his part, but he didn't have to do it and I certainly appreciated it.

Occasionally in the pro-amateur events they will have a male pro playing with a woman celebrity. Some of the good women golfers I can think of in this category are Dinah Shore, Rita Hayworth, Billy Jean King, Mrs. Bob Hope, Lucille Ball and Joan Crawford. Dinah Shore has good rhythm and Billy Jean King is just a natural athlete; I think she'd be good in any sport she wanted to try. Mrs. Hope probably took up golf as a matter of self-defense.

Many men amateurs find it a bit disconcerting to be outperformed by a woman. They are embarrassed when you outdrive them or you sink a putt that they missed. They usually have a thousand excuses why they can't hit the ball—a hard day at the office, ill health, etc. It's particularly noticeable on the short game.

As I said, women seem to have a finer touch with the short irons and when we pitch up to the green we're likely to be in a better spot to hole out than the man we're playing with. Often, one of the men will muff an approach shot and he'll say, "This just isn't my day for golf. I should have gone to work." Of course, what he fails to realize is that we are working.

I'd like to make it clear that there are very few similarities between the men's golf tour and the LPGA tour. The two organizations are made up of professionals who happen to play golf, but there the comparison ends. You can't compare the way we play golf to the way the men play golf any more than you can compare a No. 9 iron to a sand trap. You can't compare us in distance or the way we go about playing the game.

The men pros have an older organization—they've been in existence 15 years longer—and they therefore have a tighter grip on the market. Consequently, the "prime" cities, where the big purses are available, will bid for a men's tournament rather than a women's event. This means that the LPGA probably will never be able to equal the PGA so far as purses go, which we certainly would like to see. It's sort of a variation on the principal theme of the women's movement, equal pay for equal work; we want equal pay for equal play. The inequity is shown by the fact that last year I won six tournaments and about $75,000, while Johnny Miller, over in the men's ranks, won seven events and had more than four times my earnings—$316,383.

Aside from getting to the market later, I think one of the problems faced by the LPGA is that the public thinks it's a part-time thing with us. Some people feel that we're going to play a few years, then run off and get married and forget about the game. That just isn't so. A woman doctor wouldn't give up her practice if she got married and a woman golfer is the same way. We have a lot of women on the tour who are married and they play very well. We just have to retrain the public's thinking and let them know that women do have talent that they intend to polish as much as the men. It's just directed in a little different way.

With the LPGA tour covering nine months and with foreign trips to such places as Japan and South Africa in the winter, some of the pros find that they are working all year round. Many times I feel that I would like to just pick up my ball and go home, but I hang in there because it's my job. There is a difference in playing five or six days a week compared to the amateur's schedule of playing a little bit in the spring, stepping up your schedule in the summer and then tapering off in the fall. Still in all, golf has been my whole life, and although I've had some low periods, I feel that if I ever got to the point where I was just going through the motions, I would rather give it up. I wouldn't want to be like some athletes who stay around when they can no longer perform. I never want to abuse the gift I was given. Golf has been too good to me. I always want it to mean something.

For those of you who are faced with the problem of putting clubs away for the winter, there are ways to keep in touch with the game and to keep your basic patterns of timing and rhythm.

You don't have to jump out of bed every morning, run out into the yard and start swinging a golf club, but if you can find ten minutes a day or every other day during the off season to swing the club, you'll keep your muscles toned and you'll retain the feel of the club. There are even plastic balls that can be used for practice in backyards without any damage to neighbors' windows. If you are really serious about improving your game, small driving nets are growing in popularity and coming down in price.

Putting is another good idea for the winter. If you develop a good eye during the winter, you'll find that you are getting the balls closer to the pin each time, if not sinking the long ones. On a smooth carpet you can use a glass or any of the putting gadgets now on the market as a target. This could help to while away those long winter hours.

Any doctor will tell you that it doesn't matter whether you exercise in the morning, afternoon or night. The important thing is that you get into a routine of doing it daily and for a stated period, say ten minutes. That's the only way exercise will help you and it's the same way with golf. You have to keep at it until you establish your natural groove. Once you do that, you'll find that your enjoyment of the game will double and improvement is bound to follow.

Motivation will determine how much time you are willing to give to the game and the preparation to play right. If you are taking up the game merely because your husband is a member of the country club and you want to be part of the social scene, you might be better off sticking to bridge or mah-jongg in the clubhouse. If you set a goal of really conquering the game, though, by all means set realistic goals. Don't go out and say, "I'm going to shoot a 75 today." If you do, you'll hate the game because there is no possible way, barring several small miracles, for you to do that. Maybe once in 500 rounds an amateur is going to go out and shoot that kind of a score. A more realistic approach would be to say, "All right, today I'm going to break 100." Or if you've been shooting between 100 and 105, it might be better to start off with the assumption that you're going to be in the same general area, but no worse. Set an attainable goal that can be altered as your game improves.

Perhaps what you should do is select a certain part of your game to polish to perfection—like putting. All clubs have putting greens where you can spend hours with long putts and short putts, making the long ones run up to the hole, or making it go a foot past the hole. Golf is a game of great precision. The more precise you can become with any one club, the better your chances to improve your overall score and then go on to master another club.

Sandy's Suggestions Summarized

1. Always warm up before you start golf or any other sport.
2. Adopt a form of exercise that most appeals to your life-style.
3. Try to systematize your routine so you can do some exercise each day.
4. Set realistic goals for yourself and revamp them as you make progress.

Chapter THREE

Picking Your Equipment

Wн о tells you where to begin? Your husband? Your boyfriend? A relative? None of these unless the person happens to be a golf pro. Even if your husband is a pro, it might be better to take lessons from a stranger.

Husbands are not the best teachers of their wives, and I don't think that fathers teach their daughters particularly well, although there are any number of pros on the LPGA tour who started taking lessons because their fathers were pros. The Bauer sisters, Barbara Boddie, one of our rookies, Clifford Ann Creed, Donna Young, Janet LePera, Sharron Moran and Renee Powell, our only regular black player on the tour, all had golf pro fathers and got their starts that way. Many of the other women on the tour also took lessons or were encouraged by their fathers, who were top amateur golfers, but these players went on to other instructors to refine their games.

The first priority in choosing an instructor is to find someone who knows what your abilities are and how to develop them. Some pros I know just can't work with beginners. They can teach someone with ability, but they just can't do anything for a beginner. They might look at your swing and make a few suggestions, but they are unable to help you and will probably send you to someone else. The tragedy is that there are some pros who refuse to admit their inability to help beginners, not for any streak of stubbornness or dedication, I'm afraid, but merely for monetary reasons.

Golf instructions vary across the country and according to the place it is given. At a public course, for instance, you can get a half hour's instructions for about $8 to $10. At private clubs, the fees can go as high as $15 to $25 a half hour. Of course, the better known the pro, the higher his price will be. An organization was formed a few years ago where you could hire a pro to play a round and give a short golf clinic. Some of the top men were getting $25,000 for one day's work. Nothing like that has ever come the way of the LPGA as yet, but we're still hoping.

If you want to start on a modest scale, you might investigate some of the adult education programs, where golf is usually included in the curriculum. Here, of course, you'll be part of a group and you might not get more than ten to twenty seconds of individual attention. Still, it's an exposure to a pro and if you find that you get along with him, I'm sure you could arrange private lessons at his home club.

You may have friends who are good players, but they just don't have the same insight or analytical ability that a pro has. After all, that's his life, that's what he's studied for. You would not call a plumber friend who had read a medical book if you were feeling sick; you'd want the best available doctor. It's the same thing with picking a golf pro to teach you.

I'm not saying that every pro is a top-notch instructor. Some might be avid readers who are just passing on to you what they've read. I'm not pushing women professionals, although I've given lessons at times and found that I was able to communicate with my students quite well. I do think that you should investigate the availability of a teaching professional woman golfer in your area. If you should come across another Pat Stapler, for instance, that would be fortunate. I'm sure that you would find her easy to communicate with and would soon be realizing your full potential. Communication is a feeling—either you have it or you don't. If you don't feel natural—there's my favorite word again—with your golf pro, by all means find another one. Unless you can relax, you'll be blocking and fighting the instructions and your natural learning ability will be thwarted.

Your pro is important to you not only for instruction, but also for help and guidance in selecting the right equipment to best fill your needs. When golf was introduced, the clubs—they were called "sticks" at that time but such terminology would be considered the worst possible gaffe around a golf course today—were built with wooden shafts. Then came the era of the steel shafts, which still prevails although aluminum clubs have come to the fore in recent years and graphite-shafted woods are the latest thing. Naturally, there is some snobbery involved with having the newest, finest or most expensive, but when you're buying golf clubs, the ones that best suit your height and weight and length of your arms are the ones for you.

A television ad I've seen advocates going to a big discount sporting goods store for your clubs. According to the pitch, the salesmen are all specialists and know just exactly what you want. I doubt that the salesmen are golf pros out of work. The basic rule of any endeavor is to get the proper tools, and you have to have the right clubs if you want to enjoy the game to the fullest.

Don't try playing with your husband's old clubs unless you are just interested in passing time. The clubs will be too heavy or too long or improperly balanced for you so all that natural rhythm I've been talking about could be frustrated and channeled incorrectly. Your golf pro knows the basics of the grip, the stance, the address and the swing, so he'll recommend clubs that are best to get the most out of your natural abilities.

There was a time during my career when I was doing a lot of teaching and also taking care of the pro shop. I had many women who were only about five feet tall and they just couldn't get clubs that were right for them.

As a solution, I suggested that they try the junior clubs, the type I started out with when I played for the first time and are used by young girls until they are about sixteen. The women were reluctant at first, but they did accept my advice and they found that the clubs were right for them: not too heavy and not too long. Of course, they didn't hit the ball as far as they might have if they had been using a heavier club or a longer club, but they would have worn themselves out swinging a heavy, long club throughout the day. Instead of having an enjoyable time, they would have had a trying time, and it is unlikely that they would have been coming back to the course as often.

Golf pros usually use a set of clubs for three to five years, although some have favorite clubs that they have for decades. In many cases, it is a putter—something like Bobby Jones's "Calamity Jane," or a wedge that has gotten them out of the rough spots on more than one occasion. If I were to nominate any of my clubs for that particular category, I guess it might have to be the putter I used in winning the Lincoln-Mercury Open at the Round Hill Country Club in Alamo, California, in October of 1972.

I started the first round with two bogeys. I wasn't feeling well.

Later a newsman quoted me as having said that I had "bumped, scraped and drop-kicked" the ball around. But then, with my putter I birdied the 9th, 10th, 11th and 12th holes giving me a two-stroke edge for first place over Donna Young and Sharon Miller.

Except for a graphite-shafted driver, which has given me added distance off the tee, I still use steel-shafted clubs, but if your pro figures you should use aluminum, or even all-graphite, go right ahead. I'm sure that you'll be getting the best advice for your particular case. For the beginner, the important thing is length and weight. Flaws in your swing will point out to your pro whether the club is too long or too heavy. For instance, if you have a club that is too long or too heavy, you'll get the club to the top of your swing and that's as far as you'll be able to get it. The next move is for you to swing through, starting with the club parallel to the ground. The only problem is that if the club is too heavy, it's going to bounce off your neck in the backswing and not be parallel to the ground. Then to correct that, you're going to have to jerk the club to get it back on the proper path.

To the practiced eye, an unsuited club will be very obvious. One will see the club go from parallel with the ground and then drop down beneath your left shoulder, then swing straight up in the air and go way on the high point of that arc just so you can get the club moving back down. If you viewed motion pictures of your swing, you could see it yourself: It just isn't natural. If the motion pictures were in slow motion—even home movies, not the professional kind—you would be even more amazed at how awkward and strained you look—all because the clubs do not fit you.

When I speak of the weight of the club, I'm talking about the "swing weight" of the club, which is the weight in the head. The velocity of your swing plus the mass of the weight generates the club-head speed and determines the force that propels the ball's flight. It's a law of physics: mass $\times$ velocity $=$ momentum. The club weights are rated by a letter and a numerical scale, starting with A and running through E and with the numbers going from 0 to 9.

Although I shy away from generalizations and believe that you have to determine what weight suits you best, statistics prove that a club weight of about C-7 is just about right for the average woman golfer. I would say that the club should not be heavier than a C-9. I use a C-9 or a D-0 club, with the latter a shade heavier —it's higher on the scale—than the former.

Clubs also have flexibility ratings, which are important and can best be determined for you by your club pro. The flexibility ratings are in letters—X for extra stiff, where the player is strong enough to generate her own power—S for stiff, which has more flexibility than X—and R for regular, which has added flexibility to give more whip and therefore more power of the ball. L is more flexible than R and is usually a woman's shaft. The advantage of the graphite clubs is that they have greater whip, which gives the average player greater distance. Whether you will retain accuracy, though, is another matter, especially if you try to kill the ball with all that new power.

The E clubs, the highest weight category, are essentially exercise clubs. Golfers will swing them just to warm up, the way a baseball player will swing a couple of bats or a weighted bat before going to the plate. He wouldn't think of hitting with the warmup bat and neither would anyone think of using an E club for a game, unless he happened to be a King Kong. The average male pros use about a D-2 or a D-3 club. Again remembering that you are the final judge of what suits you best, I would say that the average woman would be in the C category, although not necessarily the C-7 I mentioned.

Don't be misled about club-head weights and speed. Certainly, a heavier club swung with the same rhythm and strength behind it as a lighter one will make the ball go farther. In fact, I know some people who have shifted to heavier clubs as they advance in years and feel that they no longer have the physical strength to make those 175-yard drives.

The principal difference here is that these people have played golf for a good number of years. They have mastered the grip, stance, address and swing so that what they are really doing is compensating for a lack of muscle, a slowing down of the wrists, or the like. For the beginner, though, the lighter club, but the proper one, will be better. That's why I say go to your pro for club selection. Let him watch you hit a few balls and he'll know what length and weight are right for you. You might have long legs and short arms or long arms and short legs. The discount golf store salesman couldn't care less. He won't be watching you hit balls and it is unlikely that he would know if your were swinging right or not. You're making a big investment in a set of clubs, so deal with the pros; you'll be better off.

As I've said, communication is important between the pro and the pupil, and here is another instance where such a principle applies. Let the pro know how much money you have to spend and let him do the best for you in the category. Maybe he'll recommend a basic set, which could consist of a driver, a No. 3 wood, four irons—Nos. 3, 5, 7 and 9—and a putter. Perhaps for a few dollars more you could get something better than a starter set, something that will last for years. This would consist of three woods—the driver and No. 3 from the starter set, plus a No. 5 wood—and seven irons, Nos. 3 through 9 plus a putter. That's a set you'll be proud of and will find adequate for virtually any situation in golf.

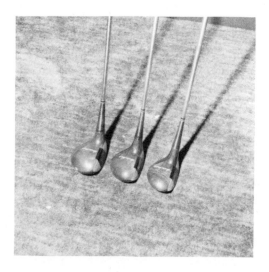

Sandy's woods are made special for her. The driver is closest to a conventional club, with the others being a No. 2½ and No. 4½ wood. Modifications involve amount of loft between 2½ and 3 and 4½ and 5 woods.

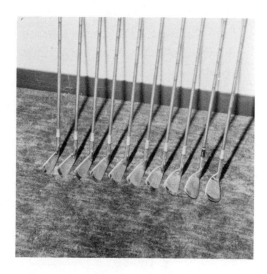

Sandy's irons, showing the gradients in the amount of loft in the clubs, ranging from the No. 2 iron on the left to the wedge on extreme right.

In tournaments you are allowed to have 14 clubs in your bag. Usually the pros will add a wedge to the ones mentioned above, and also they may have four woods. Personally, I carry two wedges, a pitching wedge and a sand wedge, and also a No. 2 iron. That's where I got my reputation for the long irons, I guess. I also carry a 2½ wood insted of a No. 3 and a 4½ instead of a No. 5.

The difference between the woods is in the amount of loft, although the driver also is the heaviest club and each succeeding number wood could be regarded as a little lighter in velocity weight. Actually, the No. 2½ wood I consider a strong No. 3 wood, with the difference being that it does not have as much loft as a No. 3, but, of course, it does have much more loft than a driver, and a little bit more than a conventional No. 2 wood. This, I guess, is where I express my individuality; if you feel the same way, which would be rather difficult for a beginning golfer to ascertain, you would be doing "your thing" if you ordered the special half-size clubs. Once again, though, I want to say that I don't think you'll find that necessary because you won't be exposed to the great number of courses and the different playing conditions we encounter on the tour.

A lot of women golfers do not use No. 3 woods very often. I happen to like the No. 2½ because I can hit with it just about anywhere on the course, and that's what I like. There are lots of times when I can get home with that No. 2½ wood on long holes where the other women on the tour can't match my shot with the No. 3 or No. 4. The same applies to my No. 4½, which, again, is a strong No. 5 wood. I felt that I could not go to the conventional No. 5 wood because it would leave too big a gap in my yardage between a No. 2 and a No. 5, so what I did was compromise, going up a little on the No. 2 and down a little on the No. 5.

One of the reasons why I would advocate the purchase of a

full set of clubs rather than the basic beginner's set is that you should learn to use all the clubs to get the full potential out of them. If your set has gaps—if you have only four irons instead of eight, for instance—there will be times when you will be either underclubbing or overclubbing your shot and this will add to your problems in getting the right feel of the clubs.

Underclubbing means using a No. 5 iron where the distance really calls for a No. 3. Overclubbing would involve using a No. 5 where you really should have a No. 6 or a No. 7. But, you ask, what happens if I don't have those clubs? The answer is that you compensate for overclubbing by choking up on the grip, that is, moving your hands lower so that your swing is not as full. To compensate for overclubbing requires a real touch that comes only after years of practice, since the irons are where the fine nuances of power, backspin, draw, etc., come in. With only a starter set, you'll always be running into gaps, when you should be learning just how far and how straight you can hit the ball with each club. Learn to play with all your clubs and find out what you can do with each one.

I have had about four sets of clubs in the time I've been play-ing golf, but I travel with only one set. That's because a full set of golf clubs and the bag add up to about 40 pounds or so and our traveling schedule demands that we go as lightly as possible. For anyone who wants to get in shape quickly, there is no better exer-cise than to walk a round with a full set of clubs as your own cad-die—not with a cart or a pull cart. Sling the bag over one shoulder and grasp the end with the opposite arm when you walk. You'll find that it is great exercise for your back and your legs, although you could be pretty muscle-sore unless you undertake some of the conditioning mentioned earlier.

Another reason for my sticking to one set of clubs is that we fly a lot on the tour—we have to now that there are so many events and at such distant points—and this saves a lot of extra weight in the plane's baggage compartment. I have one club in my bag—a No. 6 iron—that I bent around a tree in playing a difficult lie. I had the club straightened as much as it could be and I still use it. The reason I don't change the club is that a new club would have a different "feel" from the others. It would be easier to buy a whole new set than to find one new matching club.

Incidentally, the expression "matched clubs" refers to the "feel." In other words, the club-head weights are all uniform and the shafts are all uniform. Thus you needn't try out every club in the set for a pro to tell you that one length, one weight or one flexibility rating is right for you. Once the norm has been established, you are getting your prescription filled, in essence, by buying matched sets. In most cases, the clubs will last you for years, if not for your entire golfing career. Think about that when you go out to buy; it's not an investment that will be repeated annually.

Once or twice each year I change the grips on the clubs. As we get into the later sections about the grip, you'll see why this is so basic. There are two types of club grips—those made of rubber and those made of leather. The leather grips must be wound on and glued, while the rubber ones slip on and are glued. Personally, I prefer the leather, mainly because my hands perspire so easily. Perspiration makes the rubber grips slippery, the more your perspire, the stickier your leather grips become, eliminating the danger of the club slipping in your hand and causing you to take a bogey just when a beautiful birdie was in sight. Another reason I favor leather grips is that my hands are rather tender. I find that rubber grips tend to tear my hands up and hurt them.

Despite this personal view, rubber grips or a rubber-leather compound are probably the most popular. Still I feel that women would be better off with leather grips. Rubber, being tougher, has a harder feel and a grainier touch. It's a coarser thing in her hand. I guess, though, it's like dishwashing soaps or detergents: If you happen to like one kind, that's what you are going to use. I'd say the same holds true for golf grips: If you are comfortable with rubber grips, by all means use them.

Many of the women on the tour use rubber grips because the leather ones tend to get dirty and have to be cleaned. Some women feel there are enough things to be done between tournaments without having to clean golf grips. What happens, though, is that the dirt and perspiration fill in the holes on the grips, and sometimes leather grips, too, become slick rather than tacky. I've gotten around this by shifting to an all-cowhide grip (from Texas longhorns, naturally) and I think that this is the best grip on the market. You can put the grip under a water faucet, get it soaked, wipe it off and you're ready to go—no drip and no slip. You clean them by using soap and water and a towel, just like you would clean a leather chair. Saddle soap, I've found, tends to make the grips a little greasy.

But you won't have to worry about this unless you are playing five days a week, as the women pros do. Even if you play a very active schedule of amateur golf, it is unlikely that you'll have to change grips more often than every three or four years. After playing that long, you'll know if you are losing your grip, or grips.

It's likely that you'll find it necessary to clean your clubs a lot more than your club grips. The reason is that your club faces are constantly making contact with dirt and grass. Always keep the grooves of the clubs clean because any dirt in the grooves will disturb the carefully engineered design of the faces. You can clean out dirt easily with a tee and wipe off clubs when they are wet with a towel.

If you keep a towel in your bag, or attached to your bag, you can wipe the clubs off as you go along, rather than hitting 18 or 20 balls without removing the dirt from the club face. Dirt definitely changes your shot. The ball doesn't come off the club as solidly as it does when the surface is clean. Dirt on the club could make your shot slide one way or the other. That's fine if your stroke is faulty and the slide happens to be compensating to your advantage, but in the main we assume that you will be swinging correctly, so keep your club faces clean.

If a club happens to be a particular favorite, the chances are that you'll hold on to that as tightly as Linus, that Charlie Brown comic strip character, hangs on to his security blanket. I have the original wedge I started with and wouldn't part with it for the world. Ben Hogan is still using "Old Faithful," a putter that's probably been on more golf greens than a lot of people will see in their lifetimes. I also have a chipped driver that I use. The chips came about during one tournament when I wasn't too happy with my game and I took a swing at a tee marker. The tee marker didn't move, but the club was chipped. There are two marks on the toe of the driver, but the feel of the club is the same to me. I've always said its the way you feel, not the way you look, so I'll continue to use my chipped driver, thank you.

Woods and irons require essentially the same care, being kept clean and making sure the grooves on the face are not clogged with dirt or grass. The persimmon wood insert in the driver face can be changed if it becomes damaged, but this is unlikely.

Persimmon is a very hard wood, but the tops of the clubs are a softer wood that can be chewed up through wear and tear. You might not swing at a tee marker, but you might accidentally step on the woods and put spike marks in them. If they become really beat up, you can have them revarnished at your pro shop. Not all pros will do club repairs, but they will be able to direct you to a place where your clubs can be taken care of and their beauty or efficiency restored. In the main, all you have to do with woods is wipe them off with a damp cloth and dry them. Never put the woods in water since this could cause them to warp. In theory, at least, you won't be getting the woods as dirty as the irons since you'll be shooting from a tee or from a fairway lie where you're not supposed to take a divot. Those things will happen to the beginner, though, so wipe off any dirt on the woods quickly.

Those of you who are left-handed might find it a bit more difficult to find clubs because not as many are made. Still your best bet is the club pro because he'll have some left-handed clubs around, either being stored or under repair, if not for sale, and he can let you use those so he can judge which weight and length are right for you. After he's done that, he can order the set for you. In the Fort Worth area, where that frustrated lady lived that I told you about earlier, there are several golf club factories so there is no problem about getting clubs. At the present time, we only have one left-handed player on the LPGA tour, Bonnie Bryant.

The odd thing about it is that Bonnie is not a natural left-hander. She is a natural athlete, though, and was really a great softball player out in her native California. She took up golf after starring in softball, and her teacher, Vic Lombardi, thought it would be a good idea if she learned golf as a lefty so that all the power of the right arm would be there on her swing.

Bonnie has only been on the tour three years and has had her pro card only two years, but she certainly learned her left-handed lessons well. She is a long driver and certainly is among the women to watch in the future. In fact, she became the first-left-hander to win an LPGA tournament, taking the $40,000 Bill Branch Classic last year.

We have other left-handers on the tour—Carol Mann, JoAnn

Carner and Sue Bernan come immediately to mind—but they play golf right-handed. Again it's the idea of the more powerful or dominant arm pulling that club through for the maximum effect. I'm ambidextrous when it comes to writing or eating, but Carol and the others write left-handed and eat the same way. I wouldn't recommend that a rightie start to play golf as a lefty to make up or take advantage of that strength in the right arm. Bonnie Bryant made the switch because she is such a great athlete; she was batting left-handed as well as right in softball so the moves were not entirely foreign to her. If you feel the same way, lots of luck.

When you have a full set of clubs, you are going to need a pretty good-sized bag to carry them around the course. Bags for golf clubs come in almost as many styles as women's handbags; they are made of canvas, leather, plastic, or some combinations of both. Some women prefer light canvas bags that they can carry around themselves. Although light, they tend to get dirty rather quickly and whereas the initial investment might be small, you will probably find that you have to replace such a bag more often.

There are some club carriers that combine the functions of a pull cart and a bag, with the clubs sticking out of cylinders on an axle between two wheels. This is preferred by some people who want to carry the full complement of clubs but don't want to use a caddy or a cart. The disadvantage of this type of arrangement is that you can't travel too well with it. The best bag for traveling, I've found, is the large Naugahyde one that most of the girls use on the pro tour.

Naugahyde is actually an imitation leather, of soft plastic, with many of the properties of leather, but considerably less expensive and requiring much less care. The bag should be big enough for all your clubs and should have dividers to keep the clubs from knocking together. Some people like to use the plastic tubes in their bags, to keep all the clubs separate, although no one uses these on the tour. Again, your club pro can help you in picking out the right bag for you.

Aside from the ball pocket, mine has a couple of extra compartments where I can keep tees, or goodies to nibble on during a round, a hood for the bag and even a compartment for my shoes. The hood is important to us because we can zip it on and lock the bag when we ship it. Of course, even when we move by car, we are likely to put the hoods on since this protects the clubs from the other items likely to be in the car trunk.

Frankly, I feel that a bag with a hood is a good investment, particularly in these days of so many golf outings and golfing safaris. If you pick up any golf magazine you'll find at least a dozen different resorts offering special off-season rates for golfers, and the fact that you can accompany your husband on the course might just be the selling point that is needed. If you do go, you'll probably fly, and the hood will more than pay for itself.

I'm not talking about club covers, which are an entirely different thing. Everyone, regardless of what kind of a bag she uses, should have club covers to keep the woods from knocking together. If you are walking along or riding in a golf cart, you are liable to make a sudden motion that could bring your woods in contact with an iron with enough force to chip it. The covers will help to prevent that.

Covers allow you to express your individuality. They come in virtually all materials and colors and you can even knit a set of your own if you are handy with the needles. The knits are particularly good because they are relatively inexpensive. There is a new line of covers out that has caught on with the touring pros because they look so smart, with the look of leather on the outside and a fur-like inside. They slip on and off easily, which is one recommendation for a good cover. You might not think it's important, but the covers have to fit the clubs properly. If they don't, they'll either be too hard to get on and you'll be struggling with the covers when you should be moving down the fairway or else you'll be running back to pick up a cover that's dropped off.

There was a time when it was thought that mink head covers were the ultimate thing to flash on your country club friends. Mink covers are expensive and losing their popularity because of the emphasis on conservation of our wild resources. Even though millions of mink coats are made from ranch-raised minks, the general outcry against the killing of leopards and other fur-bearing animals has turned a lot of people off fur golf club covers. But, if that's your bag, or at least your cover, go right ahead. It wouldn't be right to advise you to be uninhibited about the way you swing the club but to put all sorts of taboos on what equipment you should use.

The same thing applies to balls, which, contrary to what many people think, differ far more than just the maker's name. Balls differ in many ways—even from the same manufacturer. There are some with solid centers, some with wound centers and even some with liquid centers. Then they have different compression ratings and also different covers.

The higher the compression rating, the stronger the golfer should be, since compression refers to the flattening effect that the blow of the club has on the ball. There have been some striking slow-motion strobe pictures taken of some of the top men pros hitting a ball and these pictures show that the ball is actually compressed almost flat an instant after the impact. This is what gives the men pros their long yardage. The ball takes off low, then rises, and when it gets to the peak of its flight the compressed rear portion will sort of snap back, and that's where the added yards come from.

· The average golfer and the beginning golfer should play with a low-compression ball because she just does not—usually—have the strength to get any compression on a higher-rated ball. The lower-compression balls also have thicker covers and can take more of a beating, which is important for beginners, too. The higher-compression balls—those in the 100 range—have thinner skins, in most cases, so you have to make some sacrifices for that distance. Of course, the theory is that the pros who use the high-compression balls are less likely to goof on shots and therefore the cutting of the ball will be minimized even with the thinner cover.

I'd advise you to start out using the low-compression balls in the 80 range. On the pro tour, I use a 90 compression ball, which is what most of the other women use. During hot weather, some of the longer hitters will go to the 100 compression ball, but I just don't recommend them. I can't compress even the 90 balls on every shot, which happens usually when I hit the ball off center. The reason that the women switch over to the 100s in the hot weather is that the temperatures make them a little easier to compress. In cold weather, though, the 100s are like rocks and you can feel a real shock up your arms.

The standards for compression are set by the United States Golf Association, the ruling body of the sport in America. Briefly, the compression rating involves the number of centimeters a ball compresses when it is hit or squeezed by a 200-pound weight—the harder the ball, the higher the rating. I use the Spalding Dot, which is a wound ball, which means that there are miles of elastic bands beneath the cover around a solid center. I would suggest that the beginner use a Blue Max, Maxfli or any Dunlop ball, which is a solid, molded ball that can take a lot of punishment. You can just about beat it to death and not hurt it any, which is what you want when you are starting out. Of course, there are many other brands of balls on the market, but these are the ones I favor. You can pick your own and even have your name put on them, if you want. I have my name on my tees, but not on balls. The balls are numbered, though, so during a tournament you'll know what ball you're shooting and will be able to decide who outdrove whom by looking at the numbers.

Balls are automatically inspected and graded as they come off the assembly line. There is no assurance that all the balls in a batch will be 80s or 90s and these machines apply the 200-pound pressure in the twinkling of an eye, with the ball then being routed to an appropriate place for stamping as an 80, a 90, or whatever. For example, some balls in the batch might have a compression rating of 82 or 84, but they would still be 80s. As I understand it, the process is so delicate, the spread is seldom more than four points.

Strangely enough, golf balls have not been subject to the price rises that have affected clubs or other items of equipment, or just about everything else these days. There was an article in *Golf* magazine last summer that attributed this to mass production and greater volume plus the economies that are allowed through automation. The article said that in 1964, six million dozen balls were sold for $43 million. In 1973, 13 million dozen balls were sold for $85 million. That's the Woolworth philosophy at work: Sell a lot at a small price, for a big profit. Unfortunately a month after the article appeared, the price of golf balls went up, with the rising costs of raw materials cited as the major reason.

Major ball manufacturers try to keep their prices low mainly to help the pros. That is the major source of the pros' business and they reason that if the golf customer is attracted to a discount store for balls, he might start buying off-brand clubs and accessories, too. Of course, I'm prejudiced, but I think the pro shop is your consulting physician's office so far as your golf troubles are concerned. There are instances where you might even get a bad ball or a bad batch of balls despite the rigid testing that is done at the factory. If this should happen, you'll have no trouble getting a refund or an exchange at the pro shop even if you've banged the balls around a bit because the pro will be able to tell if there is something wrong with the ball. Try that on your favorite discount store.

After all that talk about new balls, I'm going to throw you a curve by suggesting that you don't start out with new balls. Of course, for some people, everything must be new when starting a new adventure, but you can save considerable money by using what we call X-outs. These are balls that are factory rejects because the paint job didn't come out right or the letters are blurred or something. They are much cheaper than new balls and as far as the beginner is concerned, there won't be a bit of difference in how far you're sending that ball when you connect.

The pro shop also will have balls that have been retrieved from the rough or lakes or other water hazards. The Concord Hotel has a big lake on the first hole of the "Monster Course," and they say that they take about a thousand golf balls a year out of there. The balls are cleaned up and sold in the pro shop for 50 cents to 75 cents. In many cases, the balls have been hit once. Balls from water hazards may have been hit more than once, but they are still a good buy and have lots of good yardage left in them. On the tour, we get our balls free so it doesn't make much difference if we lose balls or cut them. For the amateur, or the beginning golfer, cutting a ball, which is called putting a smile on the ball, will not be so funny to you, especially when you have to pay $1.35 or so for new balls. You could use the X-outs for your tee shots and fairway shots and then put a new ball down for your putts. I don't recall ever hearing about a ball being cut by a putter, but it could happen. As your game progresses, you can go to new balls all the way because you'll want the maximum yardage on every stroke and your chances of cutting the balls will be less.

For a round of 18 holes, I'd say that you should have at least six balls. That gives you some leeway and protection against losing a ball or cutting it. A lot depends on the course you are playing. If there are a lot of water hazards or much out-of-bounds territory where your ball might be untrackable, I'd suggest that you have plenty of balls in your bag.

Sandy's Suggestions Summarized

1. Pick a pro who can communicate his knowledge to you and to whom you can communicate your problems.
2. Pick clubs that fit your physical make-up and natural swing.
3. Take care of your equipment by cleaning it regularly.
4. Pick a bag that will be big enough to carry all your clubs and have room for a sweater or rain gear if you will be playing a lot.
5. Use a low-compression ball and don't be too proud to use X-outs when you are learning the game.

Chapter **FOUR**

The Grip

PROBABLY the most fundamental part of your golf game is the grip, but it is one in which you have wide options. There are three basic grips and I don't want anyone to get the idea that the order in which I list them is my order of preference. Actually, it is up to you to experiment and to find the grip that you are most comfortable with, the one that gives you the best results.

The grips are:

1. The full-fingered grip, or baseball grip, where all ten fingers are wrapped around the club.
2. The interlocking grip, where the left index finger interlocks with the little finger of the right hand.
3. The overlapping grip, where the index finger of the left hand is overlapped by the little finger of the right hand.

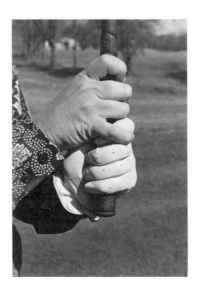

Overlapping grip, with the little finger of the right hand overlapping the first finger of the left hand (all grips shown are for right-handers).

The overlapping grip is probably the most common and the one I use. In fact, most of the women on the pro tour use the overlapping grip, although there may be shades of variations in how they apply it.

In order to learn the grip, you're going to need those clubs you bought, so why don't you get one out and follow along with me. Get out on the grass and just let the club rest on the sod in its natural position while you stand upright in your natural position, with the club supported by your right hand, down near the bottom of the grip, even on the steel. Don't force the club one way or the other; just let it sit there. When you have completed gripping the club, it will be facing in the direction that you would hit a ball since the lines will all flow together naturally.

Now take your left hand and grasp the club near the top of the grip, making sure that your hand is low enough on the club so that the small finger will be around the club and grabbing leather (or rubber) rather than the air. The effect is sort of a diagonal one, across the palm, with your grip starting at the knuckle of your left index finger.

The next contact point is about between the knuckle and the base of the middle finger, then to the base of the third finger, moving higher into the palm as each finger is passed. The club will be so high in your palm by the time the little finger curls around the grip that the base of the little finger will not be touching the club. Unless you have very small hands, the tops of your middle, third and small finger will be in contact with the heel of the thumb.

When you have your diagonal pretty well established in your mind and the pressure points or contact points noted, just gently close your left fingers around the club. Don't grab the club because that will have a tendency to close or open the face.

With your right hand, reach for the club as if you were going to shake hands with it, with your palm facing to your left. We're talking about the overlapping grip, so the little finger of your right hand will go over the index finger of your left hand, with the grip of the club resting on your third, middle and index fingers. Now curl your right hand around the club, cradling your left thumb in the pocket formed between the base of your right thumb and your right palm.

As you close the fingers of your right hand around the club, you will note that your thumb is on top of the club and that your thumb and first finger are aligned to form a V. This V should be pointed somewhere between your chin and your right shoulder; it need not be directly at either, but merely in the general area. This is merely a suggestion for guidance. If you have followed the steps I've outlined, the alignment will be a natural one and there is no possible way, barring some physical deformity, that the V I spoke of could not point to the area mentioned.

One other check on alignment is to look down the back of

For a proper grip, the club should cut across the left hand in a diagonal, from the knuckle of the index finger to point beneath base of the small finger. With diagonal established, close fingers around club.

Placing right hand on club, first overlap right small finger on index finger of left hand; then complete grip by curling other fingers around club.

Completed grip, with left thumb resting in pocket of right hand and right thumb on top of shaft; grip should be firm and comfortable, not tight.

View of completed grip with club in address position. V formed by right thumb and forefinger should point somewhere between chin and right shoulder.

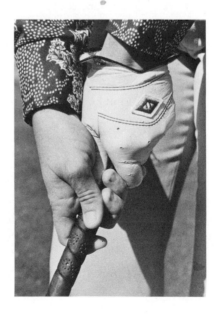

your left hand while you are holding the grip. You should be able to see two or maybe three knuckles. If you see four knuckles, that means that your grip is overpowering and you will have a tendency to hook the ball because your left hand is far stronger than your right. This being the case, the stronger hand will take over at the moment of impact and make the club head close as your hands cause it to roll. If you see four knuckles, you'd better start from scratch again and get the alignment of your fingers correct.

In the left hand, there are three pressure points or contact points; in the right hand, there are essentially two, with the middle finger and the third finger doing most of the gripping. The thumb and the index finger on the right hand are mainly stabilizers. There is no palm involved in the right-hand grip; it's all fingers. With this grip you have nine fingers on the club, with the tenth finger, the overlapping small finger of the right hand, exerting pressure on the initial pressure point of the index finger of the left hand.

Your hands are the only part of your body that touches the club, so if your hands are out of position, your club will be out of position. It is also a mistake, as I said, to try to choke the club to death by grabbing it tightly. Easy does it. Strength will make the club do funny things. If you are choking the grip to death and exerting every ounce of strength you have in your hands, the first thing that will happen is that the club head will turn one way or the other. It's either going to open up or close up merely because of the tension.

You need a nice firm grip, but not one where you are tight and tense. Tension in your hands affects your forearms, your upper arms, your back and your whole body. Just make sure of your pressure points and hold the club firmly, without squeezing. A lot of men think that they have to crush the grip and you often see them on the tee getting tighter and tighter by the minute. We call it milking the golf club. If they stand there long enough squeezing away, they can work themselves into such a frenzy that they can hardly draw the club back. Then when they hit a little dribbler or shank the shot, they ask, "What am I doing wrong?"

Women with weak hands will probably find that they have a better feel of the club if they use the baseball grip, which puts all ten fingers on the club. Carol Mann, our LPGA president, recommends the baseball grip for women with short fingers. You hold the club the same way that you would hold a baseball bat, but there are some precautions that you should follow. First, make sure that the club is sitting in its natural position behind the ball before you take your grip. Then just wrap your hands around the club, left on the top and the right on the bottom, something like the way you might have done in choosing up sides for a softball game.

Your hands should be as close together as possible and the

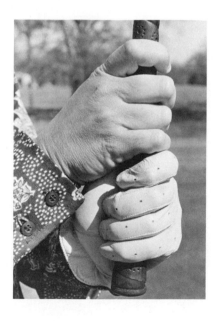

Baseball grip, where all ten fingers are wrapped around the shaft of the club and not linked in any way. Good grip for a woman with small hands.

back of your left hand should face your target, as should the palm of your right hand. The line of the club across your palm is less of a diagonal, then as described with the overlapping grip, although some women experiment and move the club more to the base of their left thumb because this gives better pressure on the shaft with the last three fingers. The same thing can be done with the right hand, grasping the club so that it rests more at the base of the index finger than in the middle of the palm. This way your finger tips will be pressing onto the grip of the club and not against the heel of your hand as it would in a true baseball grip. Consequently, you should have better control over your club.

The interlocking grip, which Jack Nicklaus has helped make famous, is the same as the overlapping grip in all respects except one: Instead of overlapping the left index finger with the small finger of the right hand, the fingers are interlocked. Follow the same instructions as for the overlapping grip but instead of over-

Interlocking grip, where the little finger of the right hand is interlocked with the first finger of the left hand. Space between index finger and middle finger is characteristic of Sandy's natural grip on the club.

lapping the fingers, put your right small finger as far as it will go between the left index and middle finger. Again, make sure your right palm and the back of your left hand point to the target.

Of course, if you are a left-hander, everything I've said about grip up to this point should be reversed. In other words, a left-hander would start with her right hand on the top of the club grip. There have been a few cases, and I can't think of the names offhand, where the golfers have played cross-handed; by that I mean they have been right-handed, but they took their grips with the right hand on the top of the club. It worked for them, although, it is hard to see how or why, but it's just another illustration that you have options in golf.

There are some pros who recommend that the club go more severely up into the palm, which means that it hits right at the base of the thumb. This is called a fisty grip, and there is a variation of it called the pro grip, which is something new among the men pros. Frankly, I don't think that the average woman has hands big enough to put the club so deep into the palm. I don't think you'll have the same feel that you'll have with the more conventional grip I recommend. If you put the club way up in your palm, you are weakening your hands and I believe that women should use all their facilities, in this case the fingers, to get the proper feel when holding the club.

The pro grip is designed for the power game that the men play. It calls for the placement of the club in the left hand straighter than in the conventional grip, with the diagonal cut down so that the base of the small finger also comes in contact with the club.

I had to smile in reading about this new grip. The pro describing it said the grip "instills a feeling of power, confidence and eagerness to hit a golf ball." Talk about machismo!

As I've said, you're going to need lessons, and if your teaching pro is one who advocates that new grip, you might be exposed to it. I rather doubt it, though, since teaching pros are a lot more realistic than some people might think. They are going to recognize your capabilities, potential and limitations. They're not going to start you off on something that they wouldn't use themselves. The pro you run into will be teaching either the interlocking or the overlapping grip, I'm sure. The pro will make an assessment as to which one you can use best and that one will be the one that comes to you most naturally.

If you go back over the basics of the overlapping grip one more time from beginning to end, it might be helpful, particularly since I want to throw you another curve at the end. Ready? Okay. Take the club in your left hand, with the first contact of the club handle at the knuckle of your left index finger. Draw that imaginary diagonal line and lay the club grip across it, hitting between the knuckle and the base of the middle finger, then to the base of the third finger and then into the palm below the little finger. Gently close your fingers around the club, keeping your thumb on the top. Now shake hands with the club with your right hand, overlapping your small right finger over your left index finger and resting the club grip on your other three fingers. Now close your right hand around the club, cradling the left thumb in the pocket formed by the right thumb and the palm and keeping your right thumb on top of the club. Note the formation of the V between the thumb and the index finger. Got it? Fine. A thing as basic as the grip is worth repeating, since your whole golf game depends on it.

Now for the curve. As you will note in following these instructions, all your fingers will be close together. Yet, in my grip, if your were to watch it close up, you would see that my right index finger is extended. How come? It's just a habit that I got into, probably because when I took up golf my fingers were small and my hands were not strong. To compensate I spread my fingers out a bit and got into the habit of extending my index finger. To me, it's natural and that's what I want for you. I don't think you'll need to compensate for small hands or weak hands unless you are eleven years old as I was. I read a golf book once by a darned good male golfer who said that if a grip felt comfortable at the start, there's probably something wrong with it. That's nonsense; if you're comfortable and it works, fine.

That's why I would never discount the baseball grip or any other grip. The essential thing is that the grips have much in common because the pressure points are the same: the three fingers of the left hand and the two fingers of the right hand—for right-handers, of course. Some women can't master the overlapping grip because their little finger keeps slipping off the index finger. To compensate for this they could go to the interlocking grip, or even the baseball grip, which they might have tried in the first place and then discarded because it wasn't the "in" thing. Most of the slippage of the little finger for women who have not mastered the overlapping grip occurs during the swing. Thus while they might be starting with a good grip, they are losing it during the swing.

Naturally—there goes that word again—the idea and ideal of a good grip is to maintain it throughout your address, backswing and swing. Sometimes, though, this is hard to do. Jerry Barber, the former PGA champion, estimates that 95 percent of the amateur golfers loosen and regrip the club during their swing. I've seen this happen myself, particularly during pro-amateur events. I might give an amateur partner a tip on his grip if I see that he has a bad one. Then I'll watch him as he concentrates on the grip when addressing the ball, but then as his mind races over the endless check list that comes from playing golf mechanically, his grip changes. If you play the game naturally and start out with a good grip, the chances are that you will maintain that grip throughout your game because you'll be doing the right things without thinking about

Repetition, practice, patterning, call it what you like, but the them.

more you swing a golf club and the more you practice the right grip, the easier it is going to become for you. The beauty about practicing the grip is that you can do it all year round in your backyard or even your living room (if you don't have a low hanging chandelier) or your playroom. Once you've mastered the proper grip, you won't have to worry about checking your Vs or anything else. The feel will tell you you're right. It might take you some extra time on the tee to run through the essentials in your mind, but take the few extra seconds, don't get rattled and don't get excited. Easy does it; a firm grip, but not a tight one. Of course, you don't want the grip to be too loose either. If that were the case, you'd get into your backswing and start losing control of the club and the reflex action would cause you to tighten up on the club and ruin your whole swing.

Even though I pick up a club and instinctively grip it correctly, just as all the other women pros do, that doesn't mean that I don't think about my grip. The difference is that I think about it subconsciously, and the long years of practice and repetition will let me know at once if I'm doing something wrong or if I should compensate in some way. In 1973, for instance, I hurt my wrist and I'm sure that made me more conscious of my grip since there was a lot of pain connected with the injury. It happened early in the year when I was chipping out of some rocky ground. I guess I should have had the wrist attended to right away, but I stuck out most of the tour and then had surgery done at home late in the year. Naturally, after the surgery, I was concerned about my grip, and I was happy to learn that I could get back in my old groove.

Still and all, playing with the injury forced me to compensate for the change in wrist strength, and there are other factors that can have the same effect.

Playing in a lot of wind, for instance, or playing when you're tired can make you change your grip. Even though I've been at the game for 13 years, I still check my grip. And, too, my grip has changed over the years because I've changed over the years. I still have that extended index finger, but my other fingers aren't as far apart as they were when I was eleven years old. Because my hand size changed and my physical make-up changed, my grip had to change, too. It will continue to change over the course of the season, which is why I keep checking it.

Sometimes its sort of a conscious-subconscious thing. I'll be feeling strong and I'll let my left hand slide over and become very strong. I'm hitting the balls well and I decide that maybe I can hit them a little farther. Then I get stronger and stronger in the hands, which is when I get into trouble because pretty soon I'm out of position. Then I have to stop and sort of take a little refresher course. What am I doing wrong? I ask myself and then I realize that I've distorted my grip in that search for power.

Judy Rankin, one of the top players on the tour, has what we call a strong left hand—she can see four knuckles when she looks down at her grip, but it doesn't bother her game a bit, as her record shows. She has gripped the club that way ever since she started at six years old and she's not going to change. All she does is compensate in her swing for the strength in her left hand. You'll note that Judy has achieved a great number of victories and considerable earnings (she's number 8 on the LPGA list) by doing what I'm warning you against. It works for her because it's natural for her; if it is natural for you, perhaps you can compensate in some other way, but the odds against starting out late in life with bad golf habits and overcoming the penalties involved are at best slim.

In tournaments you will frequently get into a spot where you'll need to hook the ball or slice it around an obstacle. Here's where a knowledge of the fundamentals of the grip come in handy because you know that if you let that left hand get strong, you are going to hook. It might be where you want to hook around a tree, or on a dogleg hole where the rough sticks out in the fairway to the right and then you have to go around to the left to the green. I'm sure you've watched some of these shots on television and the commentator has probably explained what was happening.

Your stance also will change with a hook that you want to control, but these are all gimmicks that I don't think the average golfer should be concerned with. If you can just learn to hit the ball straight, you'll be accomplishing a lot. As far as I'm concerned, the fewer changes you make, the easier it is going to be, so I say concentrate on the basics—a good grip and the proper stance and address, and leave the trick shots to the pros or those who specialize in them.

Two of the greatest trick-shot artists are Joe Kirkwood and Paul Hahn. Both started out as conventional golfers and they were both good. Kirkwood won the Australian and New Zealand Opens at the age of twenty-three and turned to his trick shots later in life. His clubs, which included some with rubber shafts, some with faces as big as dinner plates and some with crooked shafts, are now in the USGA Museum in Far Hills, New Jersey. He could make the ball go around a tree, hit it off the knee or forehead of a beautiful assistant or make the ball run up toward the hole and then start back to where it was hit from. Hahn also has a similar bag of tricks, but his clubs aren't quite so outlandish as those of Kirkwood, who, incidentally, used an overlapping grip, the same one I advocate for you.

There have been other trick-shot artists, some associated with golf hustling, which involves letting an opponent assume you are the worst kind of a rank player and then making those drives and sinking those putts when the money is put down. Bobby Riggs is known as a golf hustler as well as a tennis hustler. Riggs has been known to bet that he could use only two clubs, say a No. 5 iron and a putter, and beat some of the top amateurs, especially when there is money involved.

One more character of that type comes to mind, John Montague, the mystery man. Montague was making a pretty good living out West by playing matches against well-heeled golfers and supposedly operating under impossible odds. For instance, he'd play using a hoe, a rake and a shovel for his clubs, while his opponent used the conventional equipment. Either he had a good press agent or the columnists were taken in, too, but at any rate a long campaign was started to get the Mystery Man to drop all that nonsense and really play golf in the big leagues. Everyone, or at least a lot of people, in the resort area where Montague operated was convinced that if he could do so well with a hoe and a rake, he should be great guns on the tour.

Well, he got his chance, but he never made the grade into the victor's circle. In fact, after a few tournaments, the mystery man slipped out of sight and was never heard from in organized golf again. I'll bet he used an overlapping grip on that hoe.

But don't let me sell you on the overlapping grip if you feel your hands are too small. One way you can tell this is to put your hand around the club grip and see if there is a gap between the ends of your fingers and the heel of your thumb. If this is the case, the club grip is obviously too big for you.

Similarly, if your finger tips touch your palm, rather than the heel of the thumb, the grip is too small for you. In the main, the grips are fairly standardized, with the larger grips on the larger clubs. If you happen to be a very tall person with very long slender arms and weak hands, you may run into a problem because the standard club grip might be too large for you. Club length and weight enter into this consideration, too, so your pro should be the best judge of what best suits you. You can always have your club grips modified, within certain limits. They can be built up the size increased) by as much as an eighth of an inch to a quarter of an inch, which should make up for a lot of loose fits. They also can be torn down (decreased in size) but there are finer limits here, I'd say, only about an eighth of an inch.

Some clubs, particularly woods, come with what are in effect contoured grips. Arnold Palmer is one of the top players who uses this kind of a club, and, for him it works out fine. He says that he stumbled on the idea when he got a new set of woods one time that did not feel right for him so he unwound the leather tape on the club and put a thick string down the back of the driver as a reference line. He then rewound the tape, and he had a driver with something like an arrow or a V pointing downward. Palmer says that he found the reference line so helpful that he ordered grips made that way.

Clubs like that are on the market but most of the clubs you'll see have the conventional round grips of leather or rubber. There are even special "gimmick" grips that are guaranteed to cure hooks, slices and even migraine headaches, if you were to believe all the advertising claims, but the usual grips are the ones I recommend for beginners.

One thing the pros have to be careful about in using any gimmicky club is whether it is approved by the USGA the PGA or the LPGA. There have been instances where players have been disqualified for having more than the limit of 14 clubs in their bags during tournaments, and there also have been cases where the use of nonapproved clubs has resulted in disqualification from competition. The new graphite clubs, for instance, although widely advertised, were not immediately accepted by the USGA. This did not hinder the manufacturers from selling the clubs, however, since most of the clubs were going to amateurs who would not be figuring in competition.

If you do get to the competitive level, though, you had better make sure that you are using approved equipment. It would be a bitter blow to finish ahead of the field in the tournament and then have to sit chewing your nails while the tournament committee decides if your equipment is legal or not.

Sandy's Suggestions Summarized

1. Adopt a grip that is best suited for the size of your hands.
2. Keep your grip firm, but not tight or tense.
3. Have the back of your left hand and the palm of your right hand facing in the direction that you want the ball to go (for righties).

Chapter FIVE

The Stance and the Address

T H E stance and the address go together since both involve the positioning of the feet. Just as with the grip, there are variations and options in finding the stance and the address that are best for you. There are guidelines to follow, but they are not sacrosanct by any means. If I were to characterize my philosophy of teaching golf, I think that it would have to be the empirical method—one based on observation and experimentation. The degree of success would be measured by how well the experiments work for you.

For example, there are three basic stances, the square stance, the closed stance and the open stance. Each one is designed to make the club head move in a certain way and therefore to make the ball take off from the club on a certain trajectory. Your backswing, downswing and follow-through have to be within the prescribed limits that have led to the evolution of the stances if you are to achieve the desired results. Any deviation will cause trouble or complications unless you make compensations for the departures from the accepted norm. I'm not aiming this book at radicals or slow learners, I just feel that individualism is so often overlooked in teaching golf, or other things for that matter, that I want to stress that you have to pick and choose. You have to take the prescriptions I offer and adapt them to your own individual physical and mental make-up. I hope this will be done with the aid of a golf pro, who, if you are lucky, will guide you along the path of least resistance to capitalize most fully on your skills and talents.

This is where communications with your pro come in. Personally, I like the direct type of approach. I don't like the pro who is evasive, who suggests different things to try because he really doesn't know what's good.

This is a shotgun approach. By unloosing a number of pellets —or suggestions—the pro hopes that at least some of them do the job. I prefer zeroing in on the target: Tell me what you see, tell me what you think. If I agree with the pro, fine; I can change to overcome the fault he spots. If I don't agree with the pro, that's fine, too; at least he is being honest with me and not giving me a lot of sugar-coated double talk. Of course, some people prefer a less direct pro, one who is more soothing. Some pros have a great deal of knowledge about the game but they can't convey it to a pupil. Others know a great deal less about the game, but because they communicate well, they transmit all they know, therefore you are better off in the long run. It's sort of a chemical reaction in picking a pro; maybe it's woman's instinct. Whatever it is, make sure you get one you feel comfortable with.

In the square stance, the feet are even with each other, comfortably wide enough apart, at right angles to the direction that you wish the ball to take. Many pros illustrate this stance by putting down a golf club and having your toes just barely touch the shaft of the club lying on the ground like a straight edge.

The closed stance (and remember, all these instructions are on the assumption that you are a right-hander and will require a reversal of the terms in the case of a left-hander) is one where your right foot is dropped back slightly, so the toes are no longer touching that imaginary target line. How far do you move the foot back? That depends on you, but there are some rules of thumb, or some rules of toe, I guess you would call them, that recommend placing the end of the big toe of your right foot just about on line with the ball of your left foot. The distance is slight, maybe three inches or so, depending on your foot size, but those three inches make a world of difference in your swing, causing it to go inside out.

In the open stance, the left foot is the one that moves away from the club on the ground or that imaginary target line. Again the distance is about the same as in the closed stance, but this time the left foot is moved back so that the big toe of the left foot is about even with the ball of the right foot. This stance causes your swing to go outside in.

The distance between your feet should be a matter of comfort. There are some pros who say that the stance should never be wider than the shoulders. I feel that the stance should be a few inches wider than the shoulders, but that's a personal preference. How wide your stance will be depends on the length of your arms and legs and your torso. Comfort and ease are the keys, with balance resulting when you feel comfortable. If you can balance yourself with a very narrow stance, that's the one for you. If you like to crouch down and get over the ball, the chances are that your stance will be wider. Stance, I believe, is a lot easier to learn than the grip because we've been walking or standing over hot stoves or bracing to catch an exuberant jumping child all our lives.

A square stance, I believe, will fit any type of a golf swing. I use a stance that is a little bit open and I square around more with the longer clubs. My swing goes pretty much on a straight line—straight back and straight down, without the club doing a great amount of rotating. With my swing, a closed stance would make my swing go inside to the outside at impact. The clubface would close so that I'd either pull the ball or hook it. Whether I want to or not, that ball is going to hook because my swing will change to meet the demands of the stance.

To understand what I mean by a swing going from the outside to the inside, it might be well to imagine that your golf ball is sitting on a large X, with a line drawn through the center of the X and pointing toward the target. The ideal golf swing follows a straight arc, with your club head coming down that target line

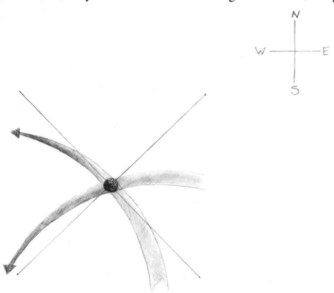

The inside-out swing follows an arc up the southeast leg of the X, through the ball, to the northwest leg. The outside-in swing comes down the northeast leg of the X, through the ball, to the southwest leg.

and meeting the ball perfectly square. An inside-out swing would be one in which the club head follows the line of the lower (southeast) leg of the X and moved through the ball along the (northwest) leg. An outside-in swing would be one in which your club came down through the upper (northeast) leg of the X and at impact moved along up the (southwest) line of the X toward the target. Generally, an inside-out swing will cause you to slice the ball and an outside-in swing will cause you to hook.

Some beginners may find it more advantageous to use a closed stance when hitting the woods, including the driver, because this gives you a bigger body turn. But how about a woman whose swing doesn't move inside her arc?—her swing is outside in. If she has a closed stance, her body is already going in a different direction from the target direction. If she accepts the advice of using a closed stance for the woods, her body will point to the right of her target, but if her swing goes to the outside of the line, her swing will go to the right and back across the line. Actually she will be swinging back into herself.

Obviously, with the swing she has she'll probably be slicing the ball, but suppose she's been playing that way for a long time. She knows that everytime she swings, the ball is going to go about 10 yards to the right of where the ideal lie would be, but there is no reason in the world for her to change her swing or her stance. She has consistency, and that is rare, indeed, in many amateur golfers. If you tell her she's going to have to stand with a closed stance, she won't be able to hit the ball at all and instead of helping her, you've done her harm. Still, she has options—the open stance or the square stance—that will work quite well with that outside-in swing.

JoAnn Washam, my roommate, can achieve the larger body turn on the driver simply by turning either her right foot or her left foot out slightly from the square stance. I guess that would be a modified square stance, but not truly closed stance, although the results are the same. JoAnn is a strong and accomplished player and moving her feet slightly works great for her. I would not particularly recommend it for beginners, however. Turning your feet could make you shift your weight to the outside of your feet, it would make you run all over the sides of your shoes, in effect. Once again, though, if it works for you, great—credit JoAnn for that tip.

When you have a proper stance, it is something like being in a box. Your body movements must be made within the confines of the sides of that imaginary box in order to achieve the best results. If you move outside the box, you are out of position and your swing is going to suffer. That's theoretical, of course. But JoAnn tells me that she started opening up her feet because when she kept them square she felt off balance. She was swaying laterally and the foot movements were her way of correcting the sway. It made her keep her weight more to the middle. That's the way she has always hit the ball so it's another example of individualism. You just have to find your own groove.

When I was working in the pro shop, I had one woman who was a good athlete, but she had started playing golf a little bit late. She was about 5 feet 9 inches tall and she had one of the most unusual golf swings I've ever seen. The club changed paths about three or four times going back and then she had a little loop at the top as if she was winding up. She had more gyrations than Donna Young on the dance floor, but the thing was she was doing it every time she took the club back. She was a model of consistency.

I got a tremendous kick out of watching her swing, but I didn't try to change it. That was her groove and she had it down

pat. All I did was change her grip and make her aware of addressing the ball the same way every time. We did improve her game,
loops and all. The reason for her improvement, I think was a
building up of confidence. She wasn't out to set a course record or
win a club championship, she just wanted to enjoy the game, playing at her speed and in her way. That's what all of you can do by
making use of the options presented to you. Don't let anyone tout
you off something if it's working for you.

Your address position will change with the lie of your ball—
either an uphill lie, downhill lie, or on the flat—but there are some
basics that should be followed. To be elementary about the address,
first set the club down in its natural position, the same way we did
when we were talking about the grip. Just let the club sit there,
without trying to open or close the face. The face opens when
the blade of the club points to the right of your target line instead
of at right angles to it and the face is closed when the blade is to
the left of the target line. Your arms should hang naturally. Now
take your grip, remembering the diagonal across the palm, the
little finger overlapped, the left thumb in the cup formed by the
right thumb's base and the palm. I don't stretch my arms, I don't
overextend them nor do I have them all scrunched up close to my
body; they're just comfortable and at ease on the club. Next I take
my stance, with the feet spread comfortably apart.

That's only the prelude to the address, which really starts with
a slight flexing of the knees. You don't want your knees stiff as if
you were going to bend over and touch your toes with straight
legs, and you don't want to stand there with knees bent as if you
can't wait to sit down. It's just a slight flexing. Here again, individuality will come into the picture and what is a slight flexing
for a long-legged woman might be more exaggerated for a smaller
woman. Your pro and your own comfort can be the best criteria
to follow in this matter.

Address position showing the club face too open. Ball hit in this way loses full loft of club and is also likely to go to the right of target.

Club face is too closed; the club is not being allowed to sit in its natural position. Ball hit this way loses distance and goes to the left.

Address position for the No. 5 iron, with the ball a bit forward of the center line and weight evenly distributed through a comfortable stance.

Side view of address position, showing slight flexing of knees; club and hands are in good lines so that V formed by right thumb and first finger points to right collarbone about midway between chin and shoulder.

The same applies to the slight bend in the address position, which is a bend from the hips, not from the waist. If you bend from the hips properly, your butt will stick out slightly, and some women might be turned off by this prospect. The idea of the bend from the hips is to keep the back straight. Everyone wants good posture, so try it.

Forget about how you look; the important thing is how do you feel? Are you comfortable? Do you feel on balance? You should if your feet are spread properly and your weight distributed evenly and correctly. Don't put the weight on your toes even in a downhill lie; don't let it get back on your heels. The ideal weight support points are between the balls of your feet and the front part of your heels. This gives you a solid foundation and won't distort the lines of your swing. If you get your weight too far back, once the club starts back it's going to pull you backward. If the weight is on your toes, it's going to pull you over, and you're going to be in trouble.

JoAnn suggests that the hip bend can be practiced by imagining that you are sitting on the edge of a bar stool. That way, your back will be straight and your shoulders back a little, giving you a good free area in which to move. If you bend from the waist, though, your free area for your swing will be diminished because the whole top of your body will be restricted.

Now when you're sitting on that bar stool, arms in a natural position and eyes on the bubbles in your Scotch and soda—or for me, my Coke—you're relaxed and at ease and that's the way you should be on the golf course in the address position; the only difference is that you're not looking at a drink, you're looking at a golf ball. In that position—on the course, not at a bar—you'll find that your feet are roughly at right angles to your target line, the direction that you want the ball to go in, and your hips and your shoulders are on the target line.

Too much weight is back on the heels; this makes a smooth swing almost impossible to achieve and can often result in topping the ball.

Too much weight on the toes hampers weight shift and can cause the taking of divots, hitting behind the ball or "drop-kicking" the ball.

Note that I said roughly, because your individual swing pattern will determine what slight changes from the norm you might want to make. We've already spoken of slight changes in your foot positions; well, the same is true for the shoulders.

Pure theorists say that your shoulders should be parallel to your target line, with the effect that a line drawn through your shoulders should converge on the target. Well, that is fine if it works for you; at least it is a starting point. When you get into your address position you won't have your shoulders turned far off your target line. On my own part, I tend to take an address position that puts my shoulders a little to the left of the target area. Again, this is because of my swing. If a pure theorist were to watch me line up behind a ball, that person would probably say that my shot is not going to land on the green, but into the bunker to the left of the green, because that is the way my shoulders are aiming. It just doesn't work for me that way.

Golf is a game of fine tolerances. If your address is off an inch, that could mean 10 feet on a shot of 100 yards. If it is off two inches, that could mean 20 feet, and so on. It's just like a ship setting sail across an ocean: The compass heading might be one degree off and the navigator might not think that was much, but the longer that voyage goes on, the wider the margin of error since it will be in proportion to the amount of initial error plus the distance covered.

To put it another way, since few of you are likely to be sailing oceans, borrow a protractor and a ruler from a schoolchild, your own or a neighbor's. Draw a straight line on paper from point A(the tee) to point B(the green); then using the protractor, mark off an angle of 89 degrees and draw a line through that angle starting at the tee again. As you see, the lines become wider and wider apart as they progress up the paper. If that's what happens in such a short distance, think what happens when you multiply the length of that paper by 300 times or more.

Actually, the way I address the ball, with my left shoulder pointed a bit to the left of the target area, is the basis for a new philosophy of golf being taught by some women pros. It's called the open shoulder address, in contrast to the square shoulder address, which is the one advocated by the theorists. JoAnn Washam is one of the latest converts to this new philosophy, which is being pushed by Gail Davis, the teaching pro at Eastern Hills Country Club, Garland, Texas.

When JoAnn first came on the tour, most of her shots were going to the right, even though she was aiming her body where she wanted the ball to go. When she started with the open shoulder address, her problems just melted away. Her hips were still parallel to the target line and she wasn't placing her feet any differently, it was just that slight adjustment of the shoulders. I guess that proves the value of my trial and error method: If it works for you, fine, don't worry about what the theory is or what the didactic instructors say. Remember my little lady with the rotation at the top of her swing. If it works, it is good.

In the proper address position, your right shoulder is going to be lower than your left, because your right hand is lower on the grip of the club. The open shoulder will also tend to drop your shoulder a bit more, which can be good, at least it is for me and for JoAnn. Of course, when you walk up to the ball, you are going to have your head down to set the club and while you move your feet into position, but then the natural tendency is to lift your head and check that your address is correct, that you are lining up on the target. When you're walking down the street with your head down and you want to look up over your shoulder, you would pick your head up first and then turn. In the golf game, however, you should turn your head to check on your target without lifting your head. Simply turn in the direction of your left shoulder and look at your target, don't straighten your neck.

This is a simple thing, but it is one of the keys to a proper alignment of your address. You have been picking up your head and turning it all your life when you want to look at something to your left, but you must alter this fundamental movement when you are on the course. The reason for the stress on this point involves matters of degree again. If you straighten up and look over your shoulder, you are not going to be looking at your target from the target line. If you merely turn your head and look, though, the target line will be preserved and the chances of your ruining or upsetting your address will be lessened.

Pro golfers, at least the women on our tour, seem to have more trouble with the grip and the address than anything else. Our swings don't change very much, but I've already told you how we can louse up our grips by trying to get too strong. The address is also a variable because of different playing conditions and different lies. Take weather conditions, for example. In January and February, when I'm practicing in Florida, I might be playing in winds that go up to 30 miles an hour. The first thing I want to do is drive that ball low so that the winds will not have too much time to do tricks with it. To drive the ball low, I shift my weight over to my left side. This alters my normal address position and that changes my swing, introducing an abrupt move coming up and driving the ball low. For winds, that's fine, but what about more normal conditions?

Then you have to start all over again and rebuild or repair your game and address for normal conditions. By early spring, I am home getting my game in shape. I let George Alexander watch what I'm doing and he can spot the problem right away, even if

Left shoulder is slightly to the left of target area, indicating an "open" stance; left foot is also in an "open" position. The body weight is evenly distributed.

Early cocking of wrists is evident as club is taken back from the ball smoothly; left shoulder starts to drop as body turn begins.

Flexible left knee begins to "kick in" as weight shifts to right foot. Wrists are fully cocked.

The left shoulder tucks underneath the chin as full body turn "loads the catapult" for the release of muscle tension.

At the top of the backswing the club is past the parallel position. Pause, then unleash. Note the coiled hips and shifted weight, mainly onto the right foot with the inside of the left foot supplying balance.

Coming through the downswing. The weight begins to shift back to the left side as the hips uncoil; left arm is straight.

The wrist begins to uncock early for added club-head speed. Right foot begins to lift off the ground.

At impact the left arm is straight, as if it were an extension of the club shaft; head is down and steady; weight is well to the left side.

During early follow-through, the head is still down; the club head follows the pro-jected target line for an instant after impact.

Natural follow-through rotates the head without lifting it. The right side of the body begins to take control again.

Club is well past parallel as follow-through continues. Position of the right hip indicates a virtual 180-degree turn from the top of the backswing to the completed follow-through.

Classic finish of a follow-through: Eyes facing the target, body balanced effortlessly and the club at rest in a position well past the parallel point.

I can't. At any rate, by the time the Texas tournaments start or I head out to California to play there, the winds are forgotten and I'm back in my normal groove.

If we get a lot of rain, I find myself moving a bit to the right in my address position because I want to lift the ball quickly and get it out of the mud. You want to get more carry out of the ball because it is not going to run as far along the ground when the course is wet, so you have to go the opposite way: You want to lift the ball, so you shift the weight to your right foot.

The lies, as we'll discuss in more detail later, affect your address unless you are at the stage where you just automatically compensate for the conditions. On the tour, things frequently go in streaks. If you're playing a hilly course, you might find that on a round of 18 holes, about 20 shots you take will be going uphill. Your normal address is off balance and you have to make corrections. But then the next day, you play a flatter course and you find yourself topping the ball. Subconsciously, you're still playing those uphill lies and the ball is forward in your stance and you're out of position. To guard against the weather changes, a pro will often hit some shots from the practice tee before the round starts to see what sort of a day it is going to be. That won't help with shots involving uphill or downhill lies, though, you just have to remember that conditions change and you had better be prepared.

Your best preparation for anything is practice and the formation of good habits. You have to practice on the course until you have the right habits and can duplicate a shot say six times out of ten for a beginning and then maybe eight out of ten as you get better and better. Think positively!

I want to stress that up to now we have dealt strictly with static moves: the grip, the stance and the address. Now we're about to go into the dynamics of golf: the swing. As I said in the beginning, the secret of a good swing involves rhythm, timing and balance. The stance and the address are designed to give you the static balance, but the moving balance, the fluidity that you need in the golf swing, is something entirely different. Still and all, if you have a good foundation from which to launch your movements and you have good position, the chances are that your swing will be a smooth one.

Up to now, I've said that the swing doesn't change, and I'd like to reiterate that before I throw you another curve. When I say that the swing doesn't change, I mean that you are not going to take the club outside one time and inside the next. However, the swing does change in tempo and in length as the clubs change. With the shorter irons, for instance, you do not take the same swing that you would take with a driver. You are aiming for accuracy, not distance. But the club will travel the same path, so in that sense the swing is the same.

You also take your club back from the ball in the same position, the hands will break in the same position, the way you start your club down toward the ball will be the same, the impact will be the same and the follow-through basically the same. Everything you do should be aimed at one final result—a long, free-swinging club-head arc. Once you set the club head in motion, nothing should interfere with the movement until the very finish of the swing. The rhythm of the swing will not change, but the tempo might change as the clubs change. Is that a contradiction? I don't think so. After all, there are slow waltzes and fast waltzes, slow fox trots and fast fox trots, but the basic rhythm is the same.

Much of the recent instructional material on golf has accented the hard swing. This undoubtedly is a result of the popularity of Arnold Palmer, who advocates that method right down to the one-foot putt. Although I would be the last to argue with Mr. Palmer,

I believe that this slam-bang attitude or approach can be carried too far. Being in the lightweight class myself and not a mountain of muscles, I'd like to say that the 200-yard-plus drive is well within the reach of all women golfers by proper development of the three basics: timing, rhythm and balance. You don't have to slug the ball from here to eternity. In fact, when I wind up to slug the ball, my timing goes all haywire and my game comes unglued.

The golden words are more important for women than for men, because men have the strength to overcome mistakes. They can be a little bit off balance, but their strength is such that it isn't going to make all that much difference. For instance, footwork and weight-shifting are important in a good swing, but a man can be off balance as a result of having his foot or leg out of position and his whole lower torso will be contorted, but he still has enough power in the upper part of his body to give that ball a good ride. In a woman's case, every part of her should be in the right spot at the right time or in the same spot at the same time in each swing. She cannot have one leg out of whack and expect to get a maximum effective swing.

If you remember way back in one of the early chapters, I said that hip movements are important in golf. It's on the swing that movement pays off, but here again women are at a disadvantage when compared with men. Because we are built differently, many women have a tendency to sway their hips—moving them outside the lines of the box we were speaking about earlier—rather than merely pivoting and staying within the lines.

Everything will flow normally, naturally and smoothly if you realize that although there are many components of a good golf swing, it is like a chain reaction, with one sequence of events easily following another. Do this in slow motion and see if you don't agree. Take the club back from the ball and note that as your arms move back, your shoulders will start to turn and your hips will follow. What you are doing is coiling the muscles for the release of the club and the impact with the ball, and when you start your downswing those muscles are uncoiling and you are generating momentum that translates into club-head speed and proper contact with the ball.

That is the golf swing stripped to its barest essentials, but let's now examine some of the individual ingredients that go into the recipe. In the address position, you will recall, you have your weight evenly distributed, but when you start that club back, you're going to have to shift your weight or you will become contorted if you stop the natural flow of movements. The weight should shift to the inside of the right foot and with the club all the way back—parallel to the ground and behind your head—the inside part of the heel of the left foot should be on the ground and your left knee turned or "kicked in" as the natural result of a full body turn. As you draw the club back, try to keep your wrists straight and your left arm in line with the club shaft as long as possible. Your wrists will break (or cock) naturally as you go deeper into your backswing.

As your shoulders turn (and I advocate a turn of about 90 degrees on your long shots), your left shoulder (again this is for a right-hander) will be under your chin and your eyes will still be on the ball. The rhythm part I spoke of starts with your backswing. The movements should be smooth, not jerky, but it is a rhythm you have to find yourself. Most pros advocate a slight pause at the end of the backswing before you start your downswing, which should be a part of your individual rhythm pattern.

In effect, what you have done is to load a catapult that is about to be unleashed, and the sequence of moves is just the same as the loading ones, but in the reverse order. You again have a shifting of weight, this time to the left foot, and an uncoiling of the muscles that will propel the club through the space occupied by the ball. The downswing starts not with the club head, but with the hips uncoiling. The shoulders follow the hips and your arms move as your shoulders move, bringing your hands along with them. The shift of weight from the right foot to the left foot means that you are making a lateral movement plus a turn and this brings the hands to the plane of the ball *before* the club head. That's when your wrists uncock or break, the result being a sort of whiplash that gives the ball added momentum.

Don't stop there, though, follow through. Again the follow-through will be a natural result of the shifting movements. The club will follow the line of flight of the ball toward the target and your body will pivot so that all the weight is on your left foot and your right toe is the only part of right foot still on the ground. Some golfers take the club on the follow-through all the way behind their backs, but I like to finish high and twirl the club so that the club head points almost to the target. This is something that Arnold Palmer does, too. With me, it is just a natural reaction to my unhindered swing. The energy I used in hitting the ball must go somewhere, so I twirl.

I also have a very early wrist break, which is unusual and that is one reason why I stressed the point about keeping your wrists straight as long as possible. The beginning golfer, I think, will not have the same wrist break that I have so it is better for her to go by accepted norms rather than a sort of individualistic thing I picked up because of my early introduction to the game. My wrists start to break right about at the ball on the backswing rather than waist high, as is the case with most golfers, even men pros.

To me, it's the simplest way in the world to play golf: you just make your wrists break, you turn and then you're ready for your downswing. As I said, though, I've been doing it since the first time I picked up a club; I wouldn't recommend it unless it happens to be a natural movement for you, too. Another departure from the norm that slender people might try to get the maximum power out of their swing is to keep your left heel flat on the ground throughout the backswing. The proper, or normal, action is merely a gradual rocking to the inside (right side) of the left heel as the backswing progresses. I know that when I lift my left heel, I throw my swing off kilter. My backward pivot becomes too loose. I lose control of the club head and my balance. However, bulkier persons, those who are not able to turn so easily, may find it necessary to lift that left heel to free up the backswing.

The big turn, the coiling movement of the back swing, is important for the smaller women, too. My shoulders turn more than 90 degrees at the top of my backswing and my hips have also turned freely. As an example of how far I turn, when I address the ball, the line from my spine to my belt buckle will be at right angles to the target line, but at the top of my backswing, the belt buckle will be facing almost directly away from the target. However, my club shaft does not progress beyond the horizontal despite the big turn. My right wrist is directly under the shaft and a slight wrinkle appears below the thumb of my left hand as that wrist bends in a full cock.

My left heel is on the ground, indicating that I do not shift more weight than normal to the right, but I can feel some pressure squarely under my right foot at this time that signifies a definite transfer of weight. Slight golfers who allow too much of a weight shift invite a stiffened and immobile right leg. Keep that right knee easy at all times: The shift of weight will have some straightening effect on your right knee, but by keeping it flexed you'll keep your swing much freer and easier.

Mickey Wright once said that she used to practice with a golf ball under the outside of her right foot so she would be sure to keep her weight on the inside of the foot when she was shifting to go into her backswing. This is only a reminder, though, and should not be taken as gospel. For instance, I think that you might try Mickey's trick a few times to get the feel of where your weight should be, but you should not exaggerate anything. If you did, you might find yourself playing with your right foot supported on just the inside of your sole, which would surely keep your weight on the inside, but it would play havoc with your golf shoes and also your natural stance. The trick is only a reminder, as I said, and only to be done in moderation.

Naturally, there are all sorts of shortcuts that work for some people and not for others. As you've seen, there are many little kinks in my game that work great for me, but would be disastrous for you to follow. One good rule of thumb and toe concerns the follow-through position: If you can count ten after you have completed your follow through and are still standing with your weight on your left foot and only your right toe on the ground as you look at the ball soar toward the target, you know that you have good balance and probably a good swing. If you can't hold that position that long, don't get mad; just start all over again until you have a natural swing and follow-through that lets you finish in a balanced position.

Sandy's Suggestions Summarized

1. Use the stance that is best adapted to your golf swing.
2. Get advice from your pro on your most effective stance.
3. Let your club show you its natural position behind the ball in addressing the ball.

4. Keep your knees flexed in your address, with your back straight.
5. Bend from the hips, not the waist.
6. Point your shoulders in a direction running parallel with the target, making compensations as necessary to accommodate your swing.
7. Turn your head, don't lift it, when looking at your target.
8. Practice to find where your most effective address position is for various shots.
9. Use a natural swing to get the most out of your abilities.
10. Take the club back from the ball slowly and smoothly, pause at the top of your backswing and start your downswing by uncoiling your hips. Let everything flow naturally through the space occupied by the ball and follow through.

Chapter SIX

The Driver and the Fairway Woods

L ET's get down to the nitty-gritty. You've picked out your clubs, you've learned (I hope) the proper grip, the stance and the address, and we've had some discussion about the swing. Now let's put it all together and start using those clubs in the way they were designed and intended to be used. What I want to do is go through each of the clubs, because, if you remember, I said that your address will change according to the club you are using and that also your swing might be adapted—I don't say changed because really your swing shouldn't change, it should merely be suitable for the club and the shot you are making, long or short.

No course I can think of starts off with a short hole. That would create too many problems since a longer hole gives you a chance to have at least two and sometimes three groups playing the hole at the same time—those teeing off, those taking or walking away from their second shots and those putting out. So, everything starts with the driver.

Many people don't like the driver and some of them are encouraged to use a No. 2 wood or a No. 3 wood from the tee. The philosophy is that if you don't like a particular club, then you shouldn't use it. That's wrong in my book. You should use every club in your bag and if you don't, what's the sense of having the full range of clubs? Each one has its own function and it's up to you to learn how you can best apply your particular skills to the individual clubs.

If you're around the course a lot, you'll undoubtedly hear something like this: "Alice hit a No. 3 iron and so I figured I should, too, even though I don't like the No. 3. I knew I wasn't going to hit it well, but I went ahead and hit it anyway." If you know you're not going to hit it well to start with, you're starting out with a defeatist attitude and you certainly are not going to hit it well.

It would be better to hit the ball with confidence by using a club that you have faith in. For instance, you could use a No. 5 wood if you like that club, or you could go back down to a No. 5 or a No. 6 iron. What you want to do is get in front of the green and then chip up for a one-putt, or a two-putt hole for a par, bogey or birdie as the case may be. Perhaps you'll have a longer chip shot if you go down the scale to a 5 or a 6, but hitting with confidence is an important part of the game. If you do use a club you don't like, that built-in subconscious is going to rebel and you'll likely hit the ball off line or top it or something that will spell trouble.

Don't get me wrong. The seeming contradiction involves two situations: A learning situation and a competitive situation. Certainly, I say you should use every club in your bag, but I don't think that you should hamper your enjoyment of the game while the learning process is going on by using the club you are having difficulty in mastering. There are several ways to overcome the problem, which mainly is psychological, I believe.

I can give you an example of that from my own experience. When I was starting out, I got it into my mind that I didn't like the driver. Every time I picked up the driver I was convinced I was going to hit a poor shot. Fortunately, I still had Mr. Mitch to turn to at that time and I went to him and told him that I just could not hit the ball well with a driver. With me, it wasn't a case of trying to stay away from the club; I knew that because it was my longest club and I was so small compared to some of the women I was competing against I had to master the driver. I said I needed the club, but I just can't hit with it. Mr. Mitch, as always, was understanding and sympathetic and he taught me a lesson that I have never forgotten.

"Well," he said in that delightful soft burr of his, "let's go out and see what's wrong with your swing." So we started out, just warming up and hitting the balls easy. As always, Mr. Mitch would notice little things about my swing and offer little suggestions for adjustments. Also as always, he would hand me the club he wanted me to use next. This is good practice since the instructor can mix up the clubs and get you to shift automatically to the address for that particular club.

At some point during the lesson, after I had become engrossed and was concentrating on the changes Mr. Mitch had suggested in my swing, he handed me a club and said, "Here, I want to see you hit your No. 2 wood." I took the club and started hitting the ball and everything was clicking—the balls were really soaring out there.

"There's nothing wrong with your driver," Mr. Mitch said after about a dozen solid hits. There was a ghost of a smile on his face as I looked at the club closely for the first time. He had handed me the driver when he told me that he was giving me the No. 2 wood. What he had done was to show me that my problem was strictly a mental one. He pulled a switch on me, but that changed my whole perspective. My frame of mind was different from then on about the driver and I know that I would never have achieved what I have if I let little mental quirks like that stand in my way.

So for those of you who regard the driver with awe and with some distaste, take heart. If your swing is correct—and your pro can tell you that—just go about your business and enjoy the game. Maybe you can play a trick on yourself the way Mr. Mitch did on me: Instead of thinking you are using a driver, tell yourself it's a No. 1½ wood. Remember, it's all in your mind.

Because the driver is for distance, a lot of women think that they have to kill the ball, swinging too hard and losing all their timing and balance. You start swinging with the weight on the outside of your feet and you tend to overswing, which means that the club will go past parallel and you'll tend to lose your grip. Now there is nothing wrong about going past parallel if that is the way you normally swing. The club could very well go behind your head and past the point where it is parallel to the ground at the start of your downswing if you have a big turn.

Marlene Bauer Hagge, for instance, has one of the biggest turns I've ever seen. Marlene, one of the top players on the tour, can wrap that club all around so far that she could look out of the corner of her left eye and see the club head. She's only 5 feet 2 inches and very agile. Her turn is so big that if she wasn't concentrating on the ball, she'd be able to see not only the clubheads on her woods, but also on her long irons, too. Despite the big turn and the dropping of the club below the parallel point, Marlene has the club under control at all times.

The big thing is playing within the limits of your capabilities. Take the driver, for instance. Suppose you can hit the ball only 150 yards. But Sandra Haynie said a 200-yard drive is well within reach of many amateur women golfers. All right, but you're hitting them consistently at 150 yards, right? So that's your range; recognize it and play with it. Don't try to powder the ball in search of that 185-yarder off the tee. Take that 150-yard drive consistently, but keep the ball in play. If you try to murder the ball, your swing is going to fall apart and you're going to be in trouble. The consistent 150-yard driver will score better in the end, which is what the game is all about.

My positive thinking starts on the tee. First of all, I like to tee the ball fairly high, because you usually get more distance than if you tee the ball low. After the ball is teed up, I step back behind the ball to look at the target area: where I want the ball to go. I visualize the flight of the ball as it soars toward the green, or on a very long hole, to the best possible spot from which to take a second shot. While it is true that the beginner should take one stroke at a time, strategy will enter into your game as you make more progress. You might, for instance, recognize the hazards presented by a particular hole and play it safe rather than challenge a pond or some tree that juts out from the side. There are some men pros who say that they have their second, third and fourth shots pictured as they walk up to the tee, but that is beyond me and I seriously doubt it. If golf was that precise, an awful lot of the fun and the challenge would be gone.

Now that your ball is teed up, take your stance and address the ball. There are many different schools of thought regarding the position of the ball at address and again you are going to have to experiment under the eyes of your pro. Much of the current literature calls for the ball to be just off your left heel at address.

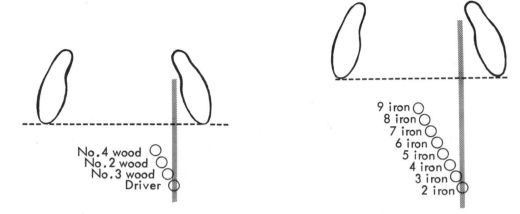

No.4 wood
No.2 wood
No.3 wood
Driver

9 iron
8 iron
7 iron
6 iron
5 iron
4 iron
3 iron
2 iron

The ball positions shown are generalized (Sandra drives off her left big toe rather than her left heel). Remember, as you use shorter irons your feet come closer together and your stance becomes more open.

The stance, as we developed, is basically a square stance, with any variations on the theme that might suit you and your particular body movements. Because you are swinging your longest club, your stance should be a good solid one, a few inches wider than your shoulders.

I don't believe in using the left heel as the reference point for the ball on the drive. I like to play the ball off the left big toe or off the left instep. By that, I mean, of course, that the ball rests where an imaginary line from your toe or your instep (whichever you find the best and easiest) intersects your target path at a right angle.

Your rhythm comes into play as soon as you move the club head back on the start of your backswing. Ideally, this should be done in one coordinated, synchronized movement, with the hips turning, the shoulders turning, your weight shifting and the club going back smoothly and gracefully. You've got to be slow and smooth going back and then you accelerate on the downswing through the impact area. You're propelling the ball toward the target, not behind you, so you don't use all your energy and thrust taking the club back; if you do, you'll have less left for the downswing.

If you jerk the club back quickly, as you've undoubtedly seen so many amateur players do, you will probably throw yourself off balance and won't be in a good position for the downswing. Because I feel that a good swing is a natural chain reaction set off by muscles, I believe that a good backswing sets up a good downswing and follow-through. It's like coiling a spring, if it is done right; the body parts that have turned or shifted will seek to return to the starting points. Of course, because you swing through the ball, with your follow-through, you will not finish in the same position that you started.

Many pros advocate the strong-left-side theory in driving, contending that you have to keep your left arm straight. This may be true at the start of the backswing, but if you look at some action pictures of the pros who advocate this type of swing you'll see that the left arm is bent at the top of the backswing. That's why I shy away from the dogmatic approach. Instruction can be taken too literally, and unless the proper interpretation is applied by trial and error or by your pro, you are going to be locked into bad habits and wondering why.

Too many instructions can make you tense and nervous, and a good way to get rid of tension on the tee, or on any shot for that matter, is to use the waggle. That's not one of the new dances, it's essentially a kind of swing in miniature during which you imitate the path you want the club to follow during the first couple of feet of the backswing. You do it entirely with the hands and the wrists, cocking and uncocking your wrists as the club head follows the first 20 degrees of arc you want it to take. The waggle not only relieves tension, but it also serves as a check on your distance from the ball. As your club head is waggled back and forth, the center of the club face should return precisely to the spot where you want to make contact with the ball.

After a couple of waggles, you can take the club back smoothly, remembering that the weight shift is the big factor in the drive. As described in the chapter on the swing, you want to keep your weight on the inside of the right foot, keeping your right knee flexed and easy as the hips and shoulders turn and letting your left knee "kick in" while keeping your left foot on the ground. The club moves away close to the ground, then moves to the inside, following the plane of your shoulders. Some beginners tend to lose power by swinging the club first and then the shoulders instead of moving as one unit.

The left side starts the movement of the downswing. You're making a lateral movement plus a turn of the hips and your hands are leading the club head. The uncocking of the wrists at the impact generates the last bit of club-head speed that gives the ball a good ride. That is, provided you have a good follow-through, which can make up for the mistakes of the backswing. If you've taken the club back too fast or jerked it, a good follow-through can save you. This is where the men's power manifests itself. They may be sloppy on the backswing, but a complete follow-through enables them to salvage a lot of yardage off the tee. A woman can do the same thing if she'll realize that she should not stop or slow down on the follow-through: Let the club carry through to its natural position, which will be parallel or beyond, and let your right side take over after the impact, finishing with your weight solidly on your left foot and with your right toe keeping you balanced.

How does one discover what tempo to use along with that

rhythm I've spoken about so much? It's a difficult thing to say, but I really believe that your entire life-style will be a key to your tempo and rhythm. If you are the type of person who hurries from one appointment to another, if you do things quickly and jerkily, that's probably the kind of a golf swing you will have. For my own part, I would classify my tempo as slower rather than faster than the average pro on the tour, but I think that conservative would be a better description of my approach to the game. I do things in a methodical way out on the course, which is regarded as a definite asset by a lot of teachers. I like to think that is a good pattern for life, too, but just as you have to find your own pattern, you have to find your own tempo. Sit back and watch your own everyday style and you'll be able to figure out your tempo.

A lot of easygoing people, I know, tend to be intimidated by new experiences. As a result, some people take up golf and try to pattern themselves after a friend with a short, quick golf swing. That's the first mistake and it could be a bad one. Play within yourself, at your own tempo and at your own level of ability. I guess that's my rebellion against dogmatic people, those who say you have to do it my way, it's the only way.

I also disagree with people who say you must keep your head still after you have assumed your stance. I say keep your eyes on the ball, but if you have a good full turn in your body on your backswing, which is the key to a good swing, your neck is going to turn as your shoulder comes around and tucks under your chin. I promise you that if you do keep your head completely still during your swing, you'll hurt your neck. It is impossible for your body to rotate and not have your head turn a bit. Notice, I said a bit, but remember our lesson about golf being a game of fractions —not in scoring, of course. When you start your backswing, it is natural for your chin to move a fraction toward your right shoulder. When you are at the top of the backswing and taking that little pause that I recommend, the only way that your chin is not going to touch your left shoulder is if you have an exceptionally long neck. But even a woman with a long neck would notice some slight movement of the head. To keep the head immobile would be silly.

Conversely, a woman with a short neck might be inclined to move her head a bit more. Still that should make no difference if she keeps her eyes on the ball. How many times have you heard a golfer say after a poor tee shot, "I moved my head"? Certainly she moved her head, but the problem is she moved it vertically, lifting it instead of turning it. The head is like the center of a circle that our golf swing revolves around. If you change the position of your head vertically, you're in trouble. Your swing will change because your pivot point changed and therefore the plane of your swing will change.

If you lift your head, you will pull your whole body up. Then the chances are that you will be able to reach only the top half of the ball, if any part of it. You'll either top the ball or whiff completely. If you drop your head, the chances are that you are going to hit behind the ball or dropkick it. By dropkicking, I mean that the driver hits the ground first and then carries into the ball.

Of course, there are any number of problems you can get into off the tee, and many of them can be caused by such a simple thing as improper positioning of the head. If you move your head left or right of the center of that imaginary circle, it will make for an improper weight shift. Moving to the left will cause you to hook and straying to the right will cause you to slice.

One common error is made when you tee up your ball too high. This could result in what is known as skying, cutting under the ball and causing it to go straight up in the air. It might travel about 100 yards, but you haven't made a 100-yard drive because much of that yardage will be straight up. Losing balance could cause skying too, but a good check on tee height might be in order. Your ball should be just high enough so that about half of the dimples, or maybe a fraction less than half, are above the head of your driver when the club is resting on the ground before your shot. That will mean that the ball should be solidly on the club face, or the inserts on the driver, when impact is made. Another good idea is to avoid trouble by teeing up on a spot where you have a good margin for error when you want to avoid a bunker, water hazard or the like.

Judy Rankin and I were playing together one time and I did the typical thing. There was an out-of-bounds to the left, and as I stood on the tee, I thought, hit it any place but to the left. There goes that subconscious taking over again. It happens whether you want it to or not. If you are thinking hit it any place but left— left is where you're going to hit it almost 90 times out of 100— and I did that day. Naturally, I was thinking in the wrong direction—negatively instead of positively. What I should have been saying was, hit this ball to the right. It's a slight variation on a theme, of course, but that can make the difference between a beautiful symphony and a collection of sour notes.

When I told Judy about my thought process, she said that she always thought of where she wanted to go, not where she didn't want to go. That sounded good to me and I adopted the same theory the rest of the season. It's an awfully good plan, really it is. Obviously, you'll be aware of trouble spots, but think where you want to go, not where you don't want to go. The first time you play a course, this could be a problem since you will either be playing blind more or less or your caddy or companion will be subconsciously accenting the negative by saying, "There's water over on the left, you want to stay away from that," or "Watch out for that bunker on the right." Forget about the water and the bunkers. Think about the green, or that nice fat spot in front of the green. That's where you want to be.

JoAnn Washam has another way of putting it. She says, let your imagination take hold and picture the flight of the ball and where you want it to land: "Imagination is a tunnel and you've got all your bad things around the outside. You've got your view of where you want to hit the ball and you're trying to hit the ball down this tunnel area."

If your imagination is geared properly, you can see the ball take off and go high and drop into perfect position. You are thinking those thoughts when you get ready to hit the ball so your sub-conscious is geared to react positively and profitably so far as your score is concerned. Imagine what you want to do, not what you don't want to do.

Last summer during the tour I suddenly decided I wanted to practice with my trusty wedge. I hadn't really practiced with the club for months and in the previous two weeks I hadn't done much practicing at all. But when I went out to the practice tee I had it set in my mind how I wanted those balls to go. I hit one small bucket of balls with the wedge and there wasn't a bad shot in the lot. I felt so good and so confident that my mind was in control that I went through my whole bag of clubs, right to the driver. The feel was there on every shot; I didn't hit a bad one the whole time.

The point of all this is that I want to stress the positive—wasn't there a song, "Accentuate the positive"? I don't want to discuss hooks or slices or shanking or any other pitfalls that you might encounter. My thesis is that if you master the basics—the grip, the stance and the address—you are going to have a smooth swing. If you don't, you must be doing something wrong and you'd better see a pro.

All the principles that apply to the use of the driver apply to the fairway woods, which I define as the No. 3, 4 and 5 woods. It is highly unlikely that you would find a set of women's clubs with a No. 2 wood in it. The club has less loft and it is harder for a woman to use. Many of the men amateurs I know who have No. 2 woods seldom use them. They'll go to the No. 3 every time and you can tell by looking at the heel plate of the No. 2 that it hasn't seen much service.

All woods are used for distance out on the fairway. Women seem to gain a sense of confidence from the chunk of wood at the end of the fairway wood's shaft. The only adjustment you have to make in your address after coming off the tee and to the fairway wood is that the ball will be played a little farther back—about off your left heel. Your stance also might not be as wide as on the tee and, of course, you don't have that nice little wooden tee to set the ball on. You play them where they lie on the fairway and that's why club-head loft is so important. You have to lift that ball out of the grass quickly.

You do have some leeway in your stance in using the fairway woods, since you can vary from a slightly open stance to a slightly closed one. But the principles I've laid down throughout still apply: Take the stance you are most comfortable with. You want one that allows you to take that big turn in your swing and maintain good balance. There is no hard, set formula. You have to find your most effective and efficient stance and address. Perhaps you might tee off with the ball off your left heel, so you'll play it back farther on the fairway. Only you can tell.

I have seen women play with fairway woods even where I might think that they would be better off with an iron. Of course, it's a matter of taste: I have a reputation for being a good iron player and have been named to the All-American team for the long irons on several occasions. It is only natural, I suppose, that I would tend to use the clubs I get the best results with out on the fairway. But some women choke down on their woods, or hit it hard to punch it up to the green. They feel they can be more versatile with the woods than the irons. Lots of women, I know, will take out a No. 5 wood and choke it down to use instead of a No. 5 iron. As I mentioned earlier, I think you should learn to use all your clubs, but I still say that if you have confidence in a particular club you should not let anyone talk you out of using it. (There's the negative again: DON'T use THAT club!). You just go ahead and do what you do best—naturally.

All things being equal—swing, lie, etc.—you should hit a No. 4 wood about 10 to 15 yards farther than you should hit a No. 5 wood. But the loft of the No. 5 gives that club an edge for hitting out of high grass, such as in the rough areas. The No. 5 is also good for getting the ball out of divots or depressions or low areas. You could almost call your No. 5 your trouble club because of its versatility. The loft and the little extra weight behind the club and the design—keyed so that the club will have a little bounce—will skim through grass or the rough or low areas where an iron might simply dig in. Another thing, grass will turn the face of an iron, catching that big blade, but it will have less of a tendency to turn the face of a wood.

On an uphill lie, you'll want to play the ball slightly forward, say, off your left toe, but keeping your weight centered. On a downhill lie, the ball should be played back in the stance, almost over the center line.

A word of caution about hitting out of the rough: There is a great tendency to think that you have to use brute strength to cut through the grass to reach the ball with any force. That's the same mistake you've been warned about on the tee. If you do figure on clobbering the ball, you're going to destroy your rhythm and your balance. Don't get excited, don't lose your cool. It is not true that the faster and harder you swing, the farther you are going to hit the ball. Your timing, rhythm and balance have to be the great un-changeables no matter where your ball lands and no matter what club you use. When in trouble, the main thing to remember is that you have to keep the ball moving. Don't get the idea that after hitting your ball into the rough you are going to pop it out or punch it out. Make sure that you have a good follow-through and complete your swing.

Wind is a factor at all times in golf, and the longer the club you use, the longer time—in theory at least—the wind will have to act on your ball. You've seen golfers test the wind by taking a handful of grass and letting it fly. When you do that, the impor-tant thing to note is not only the direction of the wind, but also how fast the grass disappears. Some golfers who smoke during a round (ugh!) claim that they get the same effect by watching the wind act on the smoke from their cigarette or cigar, but I don't think that smoke is as accurate as grass.

Here again there are no hard and fast rules for you to follow, except to realize that if the wind is blowing from left to right, it will carry your ball to the right, so you should aim slightly to the left of your target. I can't say that if the ball takes off from your club at a rate, say, of six feet a second that a six-mile-an-hour wind will take your ball ten yards to the right. It's all a matter of ex-perience and feel. You have to know what your capabilities are under all conditions.

Sandy's Suggestions Summarized

1. Don't let the driver fool you into thinking you have to kill the ball with the club; easy does it: rhythm, timing, balance.
2. Tee the ball high enough so that the club face will make full contact at impact.
3. Address the ball at a point consistent with your type of swing.
4. Think positively on the tee.
5. On your fairway woods, open your stance a bit more than you do on the tee or close it a bit more if you used a closed stance with the driver.
6. On uphill lies, play the ball slightly forward of your normal address; on downhill lies, play it slightly back.
7. Don't try to overpower the ball in the rough, keep your swing smooth.

Chapter SEVEN

The Long and Medium Irons

AFTER your fairway wood shot, you're still a long way from home. You will need a long iron or a medium iron, depending on just how far from the green you are. I'm grouping the long and medium irons in this chapter because they both have the same function: to get you up close enough to the green—or on the green—where you'll use a short iron. On the green you'll use the shortest iron of all—in terms of how far a club is designed to propel the ball—the putter.

As I said in the last chapter, you can use a long iron for your second shot, and I frequently do, depending on the yardage. One good thing to remember about the long irons is that you don't lift the ball off the turf with these irons. When you look at the relatively small face of the No. 2 or the No. 3 iron, you might think that the club needs help in getting the ball away, but that is not the case. All you need is a good swing and follow-through; the natural loft of the club, however small it might seem to you, will get the ball into the air. Never lift the ball off the ground by hitting behind the ball and taking a divot. (Remember, always hit the ball first and the turf second.) The club is made for hitting longer and lower shots. Just keep in mind where you want it to go. Think positively and the club will take care of itself.

As far as the stance is concerned, I favor a square stance for the long irons, with the ball played off the left heel. As before, though, these are variables that you'll have to work out for yourself. Perhaps the ball will be off your left instep and maybe you'll open your stance a bit; it all depends on what sort of a swing you're developing. Essentially, the swing is the same as the one you would use on your No. 4 and No. 5 woods. With me the wrist break comes at once, as soon as the club is started back from the ball. If this happens to be the way you function, fine, but I wouldn't try to force an immediate wrist break.

Let your wrists break wherever it is natural for you—if you're like most people, that will be about waist high. One thing I do recommend, though, is that you take the club a little past parallel on the backswing. This will require a big turn, of course, and that's where you'll generate your power. And, if you've had any outings on the course, you know that you need power to hit the long irons. On the pro tour, we have some women who carry No. 1 irons in their bags, but you'll probably find that the No. 2 iron is the longest iron in your bag.

When I use the long irons I have a lot of weight on my heels, not on the outsides of my feet as I mentioned in the discussion about woods. My weight is centered and I have good balance, but I don't shift my weight too much during the swing. I can get a good turn—about 45 degrees in the legs and about 90 degrees in the upper part of my body—without a big weight shift. The big

Take-away of the club is smooth; ball is played off the left heel, with the stance square; note early wrist-break, starting well below waist.

Top of the backswing, with the left knee kicked in, the weight shifted to the right, the hips coiled and the shoulder tucked underneath the chin.

Coming through on the downswing, with the weight shifting back to the left side, hips uncoiling, with the head over the ball as at the start.

Wrists start to uncock as club is brought into the plane of the target line; natural loft of club will get the ball into the air if swing is good.

Instant after impact ball starts to rise off club face, and follow-through is carried on, with body turn starting to carry club through swing plane.

Deeper into follow-through, the weight is well to the left, and the right foot, except for the toe, comes off ground as the result of natural movement.

Don't stop here, the follow-through is only about a quarter completed; keep body turning and let the club find its natural resting place for swing.

A good high finish marks the end of the follow-through; a test for balance involves holding the follow-through position for a count of ten.

turn gives me the tight muscle coil I spoke of which when unwound furnishes the power to deliver the ball close to or on the
green.

Before I address the ball, I figure out how many yards I want
the ball to go (think positively!) and then I try to decide whether
I want the ball to carry all the way or land short and run up to
the flag. This means that you should not only know the yardage,
but also the condition of the green you're playing. Is it deep?
Shallow? Fast or slow? If you are going into a shallow green, you
might want to hit the ball a little higher so it will stay on the
target when it lands. The same would hold true for a slow green:
The ball would have a tendency to stick with little roll. But long
irons tend to make the ball run at the end of the flight so it is
usually easier to play short and let the ball roll up to the flag.

All my shots are played with a little draw, that is, I hit the ball
from right to left because of the elements in my swing.

The draw is caused by the club moving inside-out and the
club face being closed at impact. Maybe you have a natural draw,
too. If you do, it can be a big help to your game, but you must
learn to control it and to channel its movements properly. Your
pro, practice and persistence can do this for you. There are few
perfect swings in the golf game, but there are hundreds or maybe
thousands of good, effective swings. It's just a question of making
the most of your ability and adjusting to your individual needs and
physical make-up.

I don't think that anyone has all the answers to a perfect golf
swing or a perfect round of golf. Each time I tee up the ball I
learn something about my swing and the game. Of course, your
swing may change as you become more mature, but that's what
makes golf such a great sport: You always have things to learn,
just like life. Even top amateurs should remember that there is al-

ways room to learn. That day I felt so good hitting the balls, I didn't learn anything new, but it was like a refresher course.

Learning comes through practice and I favor practice before each round. That is the one area, I believe, where women are weak when they play golf. They go to the course and they may putt a few times on the putting green, but they really don't warm up. You'll find, I'm sure, that you will enjoy the game more and score better if you take some practice each day before you play. You'll find out how you're swinging the club and you can leave your mistakes on the practice range, where the strokes don't count. I also think that it is a good idea if you practice a little each day, but don't press yourself unless you are serious about the game and want to be the best in your club or the best in your area. If you are just a golfer seeking to enjoy the game and the benefits it can bring you, I'd say that you should not practice more than 30 minutes a day.

Practice is what made me so proficient with the No. 2 iron. Many women do not like to use this club because it is hard to control. There must be something psychological about it, because they see the small face of the club and think that they can't possibly get the distance they need out of the iron. More mental barriers again. To circumvent this, I'd advise most women to use a No. 3 iron as their longest iron. The club has more loft to it and seems to inspire more confidence in a beginner than does the No. 2. The No. 5 wood, which has just about the same loft—well, perhaps a bit more—as the No. 2 iron will be the answer if you think you need a club longer than the No. 3 iron.

It's funny how things seem to run in parallels. Shirley Englehorn, one of our top LPGA players, is also known for her long iron play, and her career and mine have been marked by many similarities. Shirley had serious ankle surgery and came back to the tour successfully in 1972. That could be compared to my knee surgery. Then Shirley had another operation in 1973, which compares to my wrist surgery. Finally, Shirley's career was almost cut short by an automobile accident and the same thing happened to me, although I was a pedestrian in my case.

In recent years, I've been playing a winter exhibition tour in South Africa, a delightful country, but one that does have problems, as you know. The politics of the country did not have anything to do with my accident, however. I had forgotten about the reversed driving regulations there—the cars drive on the left side of the road instead of the right. I mistakenly stepped off the curb after looking carefully in the direction that I expected danger to be approaching from—my left. It was touch and go there for a while.

Fortunately, they have very good doctors in South Africa—such as Dr. Christian Barnard, the pioneer in heart transplants—and they put me together again as good as new. I won four tournaments the next year and ranked fourth in scoring average, so that should be some sort of a testimonial to the medical skills in South Africa.

The purpose of this rather long diversion is twofold: Yes, you can play good golf despite illness and accidents, and you have to watch out for the subconscious. It was my subconscious that took over in Johannesburg and made me look to the left when I should have been looking to the right for oncoming traffic. Your subconscious will take over, too, if you say I can't hit with that club or I'm going to hit the ball any place but the left. Repetition is the key to good habits in golf and in life. I wanted to stress that before we move on to the medium irons.

For our purposes, we'll regard the No. 5 and the No. 6 as

medium irons and the No. 7 and the No. 9 as short irons. As you go up in the numbers, if you remember, the club faces have more loft and generally there is less power behind your swing since you have a shorter distance to go. Despite this, the basics are the same. Your grip doesn't change and your swing should not change fundamentally—smooth backswing, good body turn, pause at the top of the backswing, then unwind, good smooth downswing and follow-through.

The ball is played a little more toward the center of your stance, which need not be as wide as when you are hitting the woods or the longer irons. I play the ball about an inch off my left heel for the No. 5 iron. A marvelously versatile club, the No. 5 iron has both loft and power. As you get to know your clubs and your game better you'll find that a No. 5 iron also can be used on dry, hard fairways where you want the ball to run up to the green.

The ball is positioned toward the middle of the stance, which is narrower than that used when playing with longer irons or woods.

Of course, all my previous statements about finding your own pace and your own natural groove applies to the No. 5 and No. 6 irons.

When I use a No. 5 iron, I take the club just about parallel on the backswing and I'll hit the ball 150 to 160 yards. Remember two things: I'm regarded as one of the stronger players on the tour, and I've been doing it for years. If you feel that parallel is as far back as you want to take the club, fine; if you feel you have to wind up more, then take it beyond parallel *à la* Marlene Hagge. A 105-pound woman who takes the club beyond parallel will not necessarily hit the ball as far as a 120-pounder who just takes the club parallel. Golf isn't that precise; people aren't that perfectly matched. Find your natural groove, your natural swing. You can set goals for youself, but only practice and the helpful advice of a pro will really let you know what you can expect in the way of results.

One caution about using the No. 5 and No. 6 irons: Don't try to scoop the ball up with the clubs; if you do you'll almost certainly top the ball. There is no way you can get the ball in the air if you hit only the top half of it; you'll either drive it into the ground or hit the ball with the blade of the club. The result will not only cost you distance on your shot, but will also probably cost you a new ball since the cover is almost certain to be cut.

When I hit a No. 5 iron, my club at impact will be beneath the ball. This allows the ball to ride on the club face, which is the way the club was designed. The club strikes the ball first and then the ground. Ordinarily you are not expected to take a divot with the No. 5 or the No. 6, but if you do, don't worry about it; but replace the divots.

Your stance with the No. 5 will be slightly open, with your left foot dropped back just a little. What is a little, you ask? What feels good to you? That's my reply, which has been standard throughout. If golf is really a natural course for women, you have to play it as you feel it. If you think the ball position should change for you, fine; you're the final judge.

A large-busted woman is not going to make a big turn because her body isn't built to accommodate the turn that I take. Without the big turn, of course, her backswing is going to be shorter, so instead of getting the club to the point where it is parallel to the ground, she might get it quite a bit short of parallel. This will not hamper her game as long as she has natural rhythm and timing. Suppose she can only wallop the ball 100 yards with the No. 5; is that bad? I'd say there are no hard and fast rules, for clubs, or for people.

There is nothing unusual in needing something explained to you a half dozen times. JoAnn Washam and I, for instance, have good communications and we can help each other with our golf swings. Sometimes I have to say something five or six different ways before JoAnn gets it into her mind. Then she articulates what I've been saying in an entirely different way and says, "Oh, you're talking about thus and so . . ." In golf there can be many interpretations to one thought and you may have to try a series of different things before you hit on the best way.

Learning to play golf with your husband has its drawbacks. Naturally, you are constantly measuring your game or your progress against his. As I said before, very few women are going to match the strength that men have, and that power makes up for a lot of mistakes. Of course, power, when not under control, also can cause many mistakes. There are few women on the pro tour who would be able to hold their own on the men's tour. Gerda Whalen Boykin, who learned the game as a caddy in Germany, finished fourth in that country's PGA title event for men, but

Gerda probably would have rougher competition in the United States. She was the only woman golf professional in the country so she had to compete in men's events.

Beth Stone, another one of the LPGA tour members, also competed successfully against men, but on a far lower level than the PGA ranks. Beth went to the University of Oklahoma on a golf scholarship and she was the first woman to win a varsity letter on that previously all-male team. Beth would be the first to admit, though, that she would be stepping out of her class if she were to go up against some of the current crop of men amateurs.

I bring this up at this time because some women might think that the difference between men and women disappears once you get off the tee. It just isn't so. The bigger, stronger males have the edge on the long and medium irons, too. I'm sure Jane Blalock, our pigtailed member of the tour, would agree with me even though Jane was named to the 1973 All-American team for the medium irons. Jane has achieved a fine record in a comparatively short time on the tour. She was rookie of the year in 1969, won honors as the most improved player on the tour in 1970 and 1971, and then in 1972 won the biggest prize of the season, the $20,000 check that goes to the winner of the Colgate–Dinah Shore Tournament. Still and all, Jane would be over her head against male company in golf.

The closer you get to the green, the closer you come to matching a man on the course. Strength no longer is such an important factor; it's a matter of finesse, skill and—I always say— luck. If you have a smooth swing you'll be able to chip up there with the best of them. If you have a good eye and a sure touch, you'll putt as well as the men do.

Sandra Palmer, one of our top players, once was asked if she thought that women were better around the green than men.

Sandy said that the only area where the women pros might approach the men would be in chipping, which requires what is called a "soft" touch. Sandy, who also is a neighbor of mine (she lives in Dallas, which is close enough to be a neighbor in Texas), believes though that women are not better than men in any facet of the game. The men professionals, she says, "are tremendous. They can do anything."

This is strictly a level-by-level comparison, understand. In other words, the top ten male pros would beat the top ten women pros about 99 times out of 100. If you and your husband are starting out together, though, it is conceivable that there may be a point where he will be beaten by you. If it happens, enjoy it; he'll probably work hard to restore his male ego.

Sandy's Suggestions Summarized

1. Don't try to lift the ball with the long irons; the club face will do that for you.
2. Determine through practice where your best address position is and what stance you should use—square, open or closed.
3. Take a full swing when using a long iron, but keep your normal rhythm and timing.
4. Balance is important for power shots so make sure your weight is evenly distributed, preferably on the insides of your feet.
5. Play the medium irons a little more forward than the long irons in your normal address.
6. Find your natural groove and learn your yardage limits with each club.
7. Your stance should be slightly more open than usual in hitting the medium irons.

8. The length of your backswing is a matter of personal preference and ability; practice to learn your limits.

9. Strive for a repetition of a good swing and a consistency in your game.

Chapter EIGHT

The Short Irons and Putting

You're getting close to home. The flag is only about 100 yards or so away and you want to lay the ball right up there for a nice easy putt. We'll stick to the No. 7 and the No. 9 in our discussion about short irons, but I also intend to touch on the wedge, which can be a very handy club in a lot of situations.

I don't know if you've ever been at the scene of a big tournament, but if you have, you've probably noticed that the pros use the putting green not only for putting practice, but also for chipping. They'll take a couple of balls and drop them ten yards or more off the green and then see how close to the pin they can come. These are the payoff shots that frequently can save you a par or a birdie. Don't forget to utilize the practice green fully—for chipping as well as for putting.

For the No. 7 iron, I favor a slightly open stance, but you can make it as open as you need it to be, I think that an open stance

does help your body to work and it most definitely helps your
hands to work toward your target. Your address changes, too; the
ball—comfortably reached by your club—would be on a line that
would be more off your left heel, maybe as much as three inches,
and pretty nearly centered. The backswing takes the club just
about to the parallel line, but here again personal factors come into
play. Some pros advocate that you never use more than a three-
quarter backswing, with short irons which brings the club to a
45-degree angle behind your head at the top of your backswing.
Still others say that the ball definitely should be placed smack
dab in the center of your stance, and they use rulers to illustrate
this point. I could never be so dogmatic or so convinced that the
whole game could be reduced to mathematics without any regard
for the human factor. That's why I say that you should take the
most comfortable stance and take the club back to the point you
think necessary to do its job.

To show you how people may differ and get virtually the
same results, I know that Sandra Palmer, for example, favors a
square stance for the short irons. She also advocates no more than
a three-quarter backswing and furthermore will change her grip
for many of her short shots. This is contrary to what I've been
stressing from the beginning. If you have mastered the grip, I say
you should use the same grip throughout. If you have to think
about a new grip with different clubs, that will make the game
more difficult for you. The natural way is the easy way. Concentrate on your grip and your swing and you won't ever have to
change. If you have a good swing, altering your stance and your
address slightly will give you all the tools you need to chop
strokes from your score.

Naturally, you're not going to clout the ball as hard when
you're only 60 yards or so away from the green as you might

when you are 200 yards away. Even though you are using a shorter club, a No. 7, you could easily put the ball well beyond your target. You have to learn your capabilities and your strengths and weaknesses. The only way you are going to do this is by practice.

Arnold Palmer once conducted an experiment. Using a No. 5 iron, he hit six balls by starting his downswing from the parallel position, six by starting from the three-quarters position, and six from the half-swing position, which would be where the club is about like the Leaning Tower of Pisa, not quite straight over your head. From the parallel position, taking what Arnold called a full swing, he averaged 165 yards on the six balls. From the three-quarters position he averaged 160 yards and from the half-swing he averaged 150 yards.

Now, I'll hit a No. 7 iron shot about 130 to 140 yards, so you can see that Arnie wasn't trying for distance on the test. In fact, he says, he never does use all his strength on his irons. He doesn't have to, he's out there close enough to the green after his drive. However, the experiment does prove my point about the backswing, which is that how far back you take the club isn't going to make that much difference. What was it? 15 yards of spread between a full swing and a half-swing? The difference is insignificant. The big thing is to take the club back where you feel it's comfortable and keep the three basic ingredients in your swing: rhythm, timing and balance.

This theory disputes one that says women are better with short irons because most of the action is performed through the wrists and arms, where women have built up their strength by lifting children in and out of cribs, carrying bags of groceries from the supermarket in and out of cars and wringing out mops. I don't dispute that all of the above functions will help to develop your forearms and perhaps your wrists, too, particularly the wringing action, but I don't agree that the hands do any extra work on the swing for the short irons.

A golf swing is made up of many things: your arms, your body, your legs. You must use all of these parts properly to hit a good golf shot. Hands come into play because they are the only things connected to the golf club. Still, you would not want to stand there and hit the ball strictly with hand and wrist power because you would be throwing the club head at the ball and getting a lot of flipping action. I could not even begin to predict what the results would be if you did that. The number of oddball shots you could make are so numerous. The whole system has to work together. Once you've convinced yourself of that, you are well on your way to seeking the fluidity of motion you need.

The No. 7, No. 8 and No. 9 irons are called accuracy clubs. The distance needed isn't all that far. What you want to do is either get on the green so you can putt out easily or you want to get close enough to the green for an easy chip. The latter is what I used to do as an amateur. I would miss the green, but I'd be in the short grass on the fringe, where I could chip up to maybe five feet or less from the pin. I was deadly on those five-foot putts and that made up for my missing the green. Today, as a pro, I'm hitting more greens, but as a result I'm faced with a lot of 20-foot putts which are harder to make than the five-footers. In some cases I'm taking two or even three to get down. That doesn't mean that my putting has fallen off, it merely means that my improved approaches are setting up tougher putts.

The No. 9 iron seems to be a particular favorite with women because of its big loft. Maybe it reminds them of a soup ladle or something else familiar around the kitchen, but at any rate I've heard a lot of women describe it as a "comfortable" club. One

The 7 iron (left) is played slightly to the left of the 9 iron (right), which is positioned in the middle of the stance.

word of warning, though: It is not a soup ladle and should not be used like one in a scooping action. The loft of the club face will do all the lifting you need.

For the No. 9 iron, the ball is played just about in the center of the stance, as if that belly dancer's diamond we spoke about had just popped straight out of her navel. Again there are variations in the ball positioning, but in this case I urge that you do not go beyond the center point of your stance—in other words, the ball should either be equidistant between your feet or a shade closer to your left foot, not your right (remember, we are speaking of right-handed players). If you let the ball get too far back with the 9 iron, you could get in trouble by overpowering the ball unless you hit it just right.

Playing the ball behind the center line in effect negates the loft on the No. 9 iron because the club head will come in contact with the ball in the wrong position—it will be more like a No. 7 iron. Without that loft, the ball is going to go lower and farther since none of the impact energy will be used in raising the ball to the intended height. Consequently, you may be faced with a shot of, say, 65 yards, but subverting the club face by moving the ball so far back will probably send the ball 100 yards or more.

One way you can check your address and stance, remember, is letting the club sit naturally behind the ball before you close up your grip. If the club sits in its natural position behind the ball, then you'll know that you are not moving too far back on it. A taller person, for instance, might find that she would play the ball farther back than I do, which is about three inches or so off my left heel. This is because I'm small and have a swing that works on an upright basis. You have to find out what the arc of your swing is and then you'll know where the ball should be played. The only way you'll know is practice.

Most women like the No. 9 for those little chips or pitches just off the green. They develop a nice rhythm in their swing and they can make these shots sometimes a lot better than any other. Don't knock it. Any part of the game that you can excel in will help you with your overall round. Another good thing about the No. 9 is that it can be used nicely for practicing short pitches and chips in your backyard, unless you happen to live in an apartment or on a postage-stamp sized lot. Come to think of it, using those plastic balls, you can even practice short pitches in your living room or recreation room, particularly if you have a shag rug (if not, you could always buy one of those Astroturf doormats). It will simulate conditions you'll run into on the course a lot: where you are about two to ten feet off the green and want to run the ball up to the flag.

There are a few precautions to be observed when making those chip shots, which we call "soft" shots. First of all, because a big body turn is not required, your feet are a lot closer together than when hitting a longer iron shot. Second, on address your hands should be ahead of the ball by about three inches. And finally, you should keep your weight on your left foot, with no shift, as you would with a longer club. As in putting, keep your head over the ball, with your eyes on the back of the ball, where you want the club to make contact. Ideally, the club should make contact with the ball just before the club head reaches the bottom of its arc. This will give the ball backspin since you will be hitting down on the ball.

Take the club back easily, using just the arms and the wrists. How far you take the club back depends on how far you are from the green and your own capabilities, which must be learned through practice. The success of the chip shot does not involve strength. The flow of the club head through the ball is the im-

Address for the chip shot, with club lying in its natural position behind the ball, the stance open and the hands choking down on the grip.

Side view, showing narrowness of the stance, with the weight on the left leg. Ball should be played just about on center line of stance.

Take the club back smoothly without any body turn. Length of backswing will be determined by how far you want ball to run after landing on green.

Downswing is made with arms and shoulders, much like a pendulum; don't try to lift ball or poke at it; loft of club and smooth swing will do the job.

Follow-through is important on chip shots, too. Unless you develop the rhythm that carries you into smooth follow-through you'll be punching at the ball.

portant factor, and you can make this smooth by keeping your hands ahead of the ball on the downswing and bringing the club along like a pendulum, with the wrists firm and straight on impact. The ball should pop up quickly and land with backspin that will enable it to hold the green. In addition to practicing how much of a backswing you should take on your chip shots, you might also want to experiment with choking up on the club, which will cut down on the distance the ball will carry. This can be done not only with the No. 9 iron, but you can also do the same thing with a No. 7, or even a No. 5, which a lot of players use for chips, particularly when the ball has a longer distance to run up to the flag after landing on the green. The No. 5 and No. 7 can be used indoors on your rug if they are choked down.

The rug also will give you some good experience in playing from a bare lie, which is very common in Texas. I've run into so many of these situations, and swinging on that rocky ground might have been a factor in damaging my wrist. I'm not too sure that I wouldn't do it again—Lone Star stubbornness, I guess.

There are three types of ground that would qualify for the conditions I'm talking about—bare hard ground, bare muddy ground and divots. Of course, etiquette demands that all divots be replaced, but sometimes this hasn't been done because the divot has been pulverized or the person taking the divot is just too hurried or doesn't care. At any rate, you are likely to encounter bare, hard ground during the summer months, when there is a scarcity of rain, mud in the spring, when the rains are generally heavy, and divots at any time of the year. All require the same treatment with certain variations.

The chip or pitch from bare ground is probably the easiest shot because you don't have to be afraid of hitting the ball "fat"—which means hitting behind the ball. Just take your normal swing, with an emphasis on pulling through firmly with your left arm. If you should hit slightly behind the ball, you'll still get an acceptable shot because your left hand will pull through and the club will slide or skid into the ball. If you hit too far behind the ball, however, your club will bounce and you'll probably botch the shot badly. However, with all the positive thinking you've been doing up to now, you know it's just a momentary defect in your swing, so you're not going to worry about it.

If the ball is lying on soft muddy ground, you must lift the ball cleanly, again with your normal swing. The variation here involves your address. Normally, you would let the club sit in its proper position behind the ball, but on muddy ground you want to hold the club a fraction higher off the ground when addressing the ball and swing through firmly.

Do not scoop up the ball on muddy ground. If you are on turf and try to scoop it, you might be forgiven by the grass, which will allow the club head to slide into the ball, but once your club strikes mud, you're dead.

When the ball is lying in a divot, you should play it two or three inches farther back in your stance than normal. This will give you a little steeper swing plane, making the club move down more sharply. After this slight adjustment, just use your normal swing, with perhaps a bit more crispness in it since the ball needs that little extra jolt to rise more quickly.

A special problem arises when the ball is lying against the target end of the divot. This means it is going to fly a little higher as it comes out, so you must take that into consideration when you select a club. It's a good idea to take a longer club than you would ordinarily use. For instance, if you are in your No. 9 iron range, it might be better to use the No. 7. Or if you are in the No. 7 range, it might be better to use a No. 5.

Since the club will tend to travel in the path of the divot, it's a good idea to check the direction of the divot to determine which way the ball is going to come out. If the divot is aimed to the left of your target, you can open up your club face a bit to help fade the ball back on line. If it is facing right, close the club face a little. A fade will give you a higher, softer shot, so you may want to take more club. The shot from the closed club face will come out "shooting" and hooking, meaning it will run farther, so you must compensate accordingly.

When you take a divot—and the No. 7, the No. 9 and the wedge are designed to take divots unless your ball sits on extra-high grass—you should study the marks of the divot. If you are swinging correctly, the divot will point toward your target. If you are hooking, the divot will point to the right and if you are slicing the divot will point to the left of the target.

The slice divot, hook divot, fat divot—hitting too far behind the ball—push divot—from in front of the ball—are all indications of an incorrect swing. This is true, also, when you do not take a divot where you would normally be expected to do so. Such a shot makes the ball go higher, but not as far as it should. Usually, this results from playing the ball too far forward in your stance. The proper divot mark should start right under where the ball was, with a fairly steep descent into the low point of the divot and then becoming more shallow toward the front end. I don't expect you to start reading divots any more than I would expect you to start reading tea leaves if you were setting out for the first time as either a golfer or a fortune teller. Only practice, your own style and your own pro can tell you the significance of your divot or when you should be taking a divot.

All of the shots I've spoken of in this chapter can be taken with a wedge, but a lot of women don't like the wedge. I think they are turned off by the look of the club, with its big face and its big loft. They would rather use the No. 9 iron and let the ball fly almost to the green and then run up on the green. With a wedge, though, you are not going to get much run on the fairway; the idea is to make the ball fly all the way to the green and stop right there.

Pros like the wedge because there are so many times that you need a shot requiring a lot of height in a relatively short distance— to get over a bunker, say, or to clear a tree. You need the height, but you want the ball to stop on the green. You can achieve that effect with a No. 9 from a long distance, but not up close, say, about 65 yards. When you are even closer than that, you can open up the face of the wedge and cut the legs out from under the golf ball. That means putting backspin on the ball so that when it lands, it will "dance on the green," start spinning back in the direction of its flight.

To me, the wedge is a great club for accuracy (remember those two wedge shots for eagles in the 1973 Lincoln-Mercury?) and I don't think women should let the appearance of the club set up any prejudices in their minds. You can use the wedge profitably for sand shots, trouble shots or from the fairway when you want that ball to get close to the pin, say, within a 15-foot radius. The big thing, as with all the clubs, is to learn what your maximum range is and then adjust your swing accordingly. For instance, if my top range for a wedge were 75 yards, I would never try to hit the ball more than 65 yards, because if you go all out on a swing, you are going to have to sacrifice accuracy and then you defeat the whole purpose of the wedge.

Lots of times you might be playing a short par-5 hole with the wedge on your third shot. You have an opportunity to make a birdie and pick up a stroke or you've gotten into trouble and with the wedge in your hand you have a chance to knock it up close and save your par. Many people feel that they have to go all out with their swing when using the wedge, and that's where the trouble starts. Because of the big face, the angle and the big sole of the club, a poor swing can open the way for a multitude of miseries. One of the most common errors would be the fat shot, hitting the ground first and the ball second and taking a big chunk of real estate along the way. Another common error would be hitting the ball with the lip of the club, which would cause the ball to take off about knee high (we say quail high in Texas) and traveling about 30 or 40 yards farther than you want it to go.

You can master the wedge if you have mastered the golf swing. All you need do is take an open stance, with the ball about in the midpoint at address. You don't want a big swing, in fact, you can choke down on the club if you like, this will help to make your swing more compact.

Your backswing, the degree that your feet are open and the amount of choke you'll put on the club depend on your own personal needs and tastes. In fact, you can open your stance even more than you've done with any of the other clubs so long as you keep your flight path and the club head moving toward the target. The opening of your stance and a slight opening of the club face will help you to gain more loft and more backspin since those ridges will be cutting across the ball's dimples on impact at an angle. It's sort of like hitting a table tennis ball with a sandpaper paddle—by using a slashing motion you get both a forward thrust and spin.

Most of all, you want to be sure that the stance you take is a comfortable one. If it isn't, that old subconscious will come into play and there will be a muscle revolt that will work toward relieving the cramped position you are in, and your swing will go haywire. You want to make sure that your weight is evenly distributed between the balls of your feet and your heels. Take the club back in one motion—I definitely don't think you should go beyond the parallel point on the backswing and really feel that the limit should be a little short of parallel, but you be the judge.

The pitching wedge can be used for getting out of sand. But it must be a clean shot, where the ball is sitting fairly high, not buried, and you have to know what you are doing. Do not try to blast out of the trap with a pitching wedge. The sand wedge is the special club for that situation. The chief difference between the two clubs is that the pitching wedge has a flat sole and the sand wedge has a rounded sole so it will move through the sand more easily and with less resistance. I use a pitching wedge to get out of traps a lot of times, but I don't take a lot of sand—it's just sort of a soft pitch. You can use the pitching wedge on hard sand, but for soft sand I would advise that you get a sand wedge, where the rounded bottom of the club will make it bounce through the sand.

Many bunkers today have lips on them where grass grows over the sand, so you often need a lot of loft in a hurry. To me, the trap shot is the most difficult one in golf because I don't consider myself a good bunker player. If you get into a trap, the first thing you have to do is survey the situation: Is the sand dry or wet? Is the ball buried or sitting on top? This will determine whether you can just pitch the ball out or if you have to blast your way out.

In blasting out, you want to make sure that you have a good, firm foundation. This means moving your feet to anchor them in the sand. Since this will shorten your body in relation to your normal swing, you should also shorten up on your club a bit. The address should have the ball about centered, with a good open

Address position in a trap, with the feet dug in solidly to give a good plat-form for swing; club sits normally behind ball to show loft.

Note relatively narrow stance (about as wide as shoulders) and open posi-tion of left foot; club is taken back smoothly, ball nearly centered.

Knee and hip movements are used in back-swing, length of which depends on whether sand is wet or dry and how far from the pin the ball is hit.

Top of backswing (about a three-quarter swing here), with eyes on a spot behind the ball where you want club to enter sand and carry ball to green.

Explosion! Ball rides on a cushion of sand up to the green. Don't rush your downstroke; hit through the ball firmly with weight shifting to left.

Follow-through assures you of proper cut on the ball, which gives added backspin. This can be achieved by opening the face of the club slightly.

Completion of follow-through, with weight fully on left foot and right serving merely as balance. Club finishes high as eyes watch ball's flight.

stance and the club face open. Ideally, you want to hit behind the ball and follow through so that you will carry the ball on a cushion of sand right up to the green. To accomplish this, you should aim at a point behind the ball, an inch or two or three. How far will depend on the position of the ball, the condition of the sand, whether it is wet or dry, and how far you want the ball to go after leaving the trap. Dry sand will give more, and you can usually hit well behind the ball to get it out. You also can hit closer to the ball but with less power in dry sand.

The open stance and the open club face will give your swing an outside-in motion on the trap shot and this helps to slide the club under the ball. Start your swing by taking your club back smoothly, cocking your wrists a bit earlier than on other shots (this is where my early wrist break comes in handy). Your weight is on your left foot. You do not need a big pivot; keep your upper body relaxed and your knees flexible, because you will need a good hip turn to assure a smooth follow-through. As you start your downswing with your usual fluid motion, start your hips moving and keep them moving as you slide the club under the ball. The hip turn will assure that you make contact with the sand with the club face open; if you just use your arms and hands to move the club toward the target, the club face would be closed at impact and would decelerate and bury deep in the sand. This is a common fault among women golfers: They think that all they have to do is hit the sand and stop there. Remember to avoid too square a stance and a square club face at the address. If you don't follow through, both the club and the ball will probably stop in the sand.

Many people say that the biggest problem about the sand trap is psychological and I wonder if that isn't true for me. If I do have any hangups about sand, it can probably be traced back to 1962 to the Waterloo, Iowa, Open. I was one of the favorites in the field and had a good first round and felt good about playing. The second day, I got into a trap, but it didn't bother me. I dug in just as I've explained to you and took my swing. It was a good swing, too, but the club stopped in the sand because it had hit a buried pipe. I vibrated all over, but I finished the round. That night my vision began to blur and I got to a doctor fast. I was in traction in the hospital for two months and out of competition for six months. I often wonder where I'd be if it wasn't for all those injuries, but I really can't complain.

If you get into a trap, just keep your head and remember your rhythm, balance and timing. On wet sand, you should open your stance even more than when playing out of dry sand—as much as 45 degrees from the target line. You also should hit closer to the ball, perhaps an inch behind it, since there will be more resistance in wet sand. Of course, when the sand is wet, the chances are that the ball will sit higher in the trap because the compacted sand offers more resistance when the ball lands. At any rate, survey the situation and take the appropriate action. Aside from the extra opening of the stance, the shot is the same as from dry sand, with the exception that you should grip the club a bit more tightly to assure control since wet sand will resist the impact more. Make a careful judgment of the distance from the bunker to the flag. It makes no sense to hit the ball from a trap on the left side to one on the right side and you won't do this if you've mastered your swing, taken your practice and followed the advice of your pro.

And if you have done all that, the ball should be sitting up there nice and close to the pin just waiting to be holed out. Before we proceed to putting, though, I want to finish with the wedges. Which one should you buy, the pitching wedge or the sand wedge? If you're an accomplished player, I'd say buy them both for your set. If you're a beginner, I think I would lean toward the sand wedge since you'll probably be in trouble more often than you'll be shooting for birdies or eagles. As your game progresses, though, I certainly would advise you to get a pitching wedge. It's a great club for accuracy.

Of course, the accuracy of the wedge and the accuracy of the putter are two different things. In putting, you are dealing with a very small area, a matter of inches. After all the ground you've traveled to get to the putting position, you might think that the hardest part is over, but many people find putting one of the most difficult parts of the game. The putt is the payoff in golf; unless you can putt well, the rest is merely exercise.

Throughout the book I've been stressing an individual approach to golf but putting requires even more of an individualistic approach. It starts right with the selection of a putter. There are four basic styles to choose from: the mallet type, which resembles a

Left to right: Mallet head, ping (sometimes called a gooseneck putter), blade and bull's-eye putters, the four most commonly used by pros and amateurs.

smaller version of a driver, but with a head of metal; the blade type, which will be like the other irons in your set but with a straight face; the bullseye type, which I use, a center-shafted club with a narrow face; and the ping type, which is something like a mallet with the back half cut down so it will not be so heavy.

No single set of rules applies to putting. Whatever works best for you is the key to putting. We've stressed the basic grip, stance and address on the other clubs, but with putting people assume all sorts of grips, stances and addresses. I have seen good golfers sink 30-footers by leaning way over the ball with their elbows way out as if they were bent over in prayer. I remember, too, one golfer who used to line up facing the hole, with his feet parallel to the line of the putt, and swinging a putter that looked like a modified croquet mallet between his legs. The stances might look funny and ungainly, but if they work, don't knock it.

Your putter doesn't have to match your set, just as your movements on the green don't have to match your movements on the tee or the fairways. You might want a light putter or a heavy putter. The only way you'll know is by experimenting. Some people might want to carry a light putter for fast greens and a heavy putter for slow greens, but I think that is a needless complication. Just find a putter you like and you can adapt it to various greens.

It is still important, however, to assume some sort of a good grip to make sure that the hands stay together and work together. I use a reverse overlapping grip, which means I put my right hand on the putter, then I put three fingers of the left hand on the grip and the first finger of the left hand over the outside of the right little finger. That's comfortable for me, but may not be for you. Among the top putters on the tour there is a wide disparity in their putting grips.

Sandy uses a reverse overlap grip for putting. Only difference in this grip and normal overlapping grip is that the index finger of the left hand overlaps the third finger of right instead of right small finger overlapping index finger of left hand.

Putting grip in address position. Back of the left hand and the palm of the right should be facing target; note thumb-and-index-finger V.

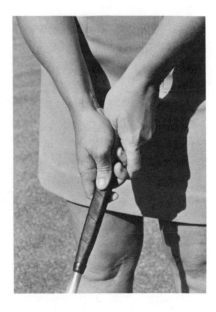

Eyes over ball, weight evenly distributed, knees flexible, and concentration evident; feet are square to the target line that ball will take.

Backswing in putting is just as important as on long shots; smoothness and fluidity of motion pays off; don't lift club on the backswing.

Putting is a smooth, relaxed stroke, with the body and head remaining steady and the arms, shoulders and hands working together like a Y.

A good follow-through will prevent you from easing into the ball, which is a common mistake among golfers. Club should be moving along target line.

Head turns naturally as follow-through is completed. Follow-through should at least equal length of backswing; many putts are missed for lack of a sufficient swing rather than from any misdirection in the line of roll.

Kathy Whitworth, the All-American with the putter, uses the ordinary overlapping grip. Judy Rankin, who has done a good share of winning, uses the interlocking grip. JoAnn Washman uses a ten-finger grip which she carries through her game. Pam Barnett uses a cross-handed overlap, with her right hand on top of the shaft.

One thing you should do is try to establish some target lines that you can line up with the hole. On the hands, I suggest that you have the back of your left hand and the front of your right hand pointing toward the pin (don't forget, this is for right-handers). You also should have some reference point with your feet, usually at right angles to your target line. Still, you have to find your own way on the greens, just as I did when I was a kid and putting pigeon-toed.

I was badly pigeon-toed, which is not as big a handicap as it might seem because your knees go together and lock your body in place. That stance keeps you from moving, which is important when putting. But I was never comfortable and my putting really improved when I got over being pigeon-toed and started to relax more on the greens. How much have I improved? Well, I won the U.S. Open last year with a 15-foot birdie putt on the last hole, which was nice, but the zinger came on the next to last hole: I sank a 70-footer for a birdie there.

Whether you stand pigeon-toed or however you address the ball when putting, your eyes should be over the ball, your body should be still and your head should be still. Oh, your head will turn slightly as you look at the target but not as much as it does out on the course or the tee. You're only looking a short distance, so don't exaggerate any of your movements. A common mistake that people make is that they try to follow the putter with their eyes when they take the blade back for the putt. This causes them to take their eyes off the ball and probably move their heads. Check two things: whether your body is moving and whether your eyes are moving; they both should be still.

Look at what you want to hit, which for most people is the back of the ball. Some people might look at the top of the ball and they may be the kind of golfer who will roll the putter over the top of the ball to get some overspin on it. Well, that's fine, if that's their style. But if you want to hit the back of the ball and you look at the top, with the aid of your subconscious you'll top the ball and probably muff the shot. This happens even among the pros. Signa Hudson, one of the tour members, once missed a two-inch putt. That's usually a "gimme" in a friendly game, but Signa missed and she calls that her most amusing experience. It might not have been so funny if $3,000 had been riding on the putt, as is often the case in tour finals.

Some pros advocate a putting technique in which the wrists snap at impact with the ball. I use a method that calls for the wrists to stay firm at impact. My shoulders, arms and hands work together as a unit—a Y formation. While my body and head remain steady, my shoulders and arms (the top of the Y) swing back and follow through the ball in a compact swing, which I feel has better accuracy than the wrist-break technique.

You also can use a combination of the two methods, breaking your wrists at the ball in the backswing and then moving your shoulders and arms as a unit in taking the club back with cocked wrists and breaking again at impact. The most important thing is to keep the blade of the putter square to the target line. You also should have the back of the left hand and the palm of the right hand facing the target. Some women who putt with a lot of shoulder motion find it useful to spread their hands on the shaft of the club, thus eliminating any wrist action and preventing them from turning the blade of the putter with an independent arm motion. They putt with sort of a sweeping motion from the shoulder, as if they were using a short broom.

Pam Barnett, who is considered among the top putters on the tour, says that her cross-handed grip helps her control her backswing and prevents her from easing into the ball, which is a very common mistake. You should make sure that the putter is accelerating upon impact and you can do this by keeping in mind that you must follow through on a putt just as in any other shot. Another common fault is taking a sloppy backswing and then jabbing at the ball to compensate. The putt should be a fluid motion, with the putter kept close to the ground and the ball struck smoothly and sharply. Many pros believe that more putts are missed because of a lack of a sufficient swing than because of misdirection. Practice and the confidence that comes with practice can help you overcome this problem.

On long putts—those of 60 feet or so—try to envision the hole as a large circle around the cup. If you can't hit the bullseye you can at least get down in two. You have to lengthen your backswing on the long putts, and some pros advocate an "inside, inside" movement, taking the club back not straight as on short putts, but just slightly to the inside (remember that X we talked about on the drive?) and then hitting straight through the ball and letting the club move inside again on the follow-through.

As a beginner, you may have trouble judging how far back you should take the club to putt. Again this will come to you only through much practice, but there is a rule of thumb that can help you in starting out. Simply stated, the rule is that you should not take the putter back from the ball more than one inch for each foot that the ball will have to travel. Thus, if you have a five-footer, you'll take the club back only five inches, come through the ball and then turn your head to see (you hope) the ball drop into the cup. Your putting rhythm should be about the same tempo as your regular golf swing. If you have a nice easy swing, you will have a nice easy putting touch; if you are nervous and jumpy, your golf swing will reflect it and it will take you about five shots to get down when you should have holed out in two at the most.

Don't try to steer the ball by opening or closing the club face; that is almost certain to make the putt get off line. Perspective is important to putting. Everyone, as you know, has a dominant eye, and this is the eye that you should use in lining up your putts. The dominant eye can affect your stance in putting.

If you are "right-eyed" when you address the ball, you might want to open up your stance a bit more so that when you turn your head to line up the ball with the target, you can get your head all the way under so your right eye can line up the hole and co-ordinate with your left eye. If your stance is closed and you just turn your head slightly, you're not getting the proper perspective since you're only looking at the hole with your left eye. Of course, if your left eye is your dominant eye, you can look that way. You have to learn which way your eyes work and then you'll know which way to look for the putting line.

I play the ball well forward on putts, as I do with most of my shots, as you've noticed. That is following a pattern, which is very important in golf. I would advise you to follow a pattern if you can; if you can't you probably aren't letting yourself relax. If you do relax, you'll get into a natural tempo and rhythm that probably matches your life-style.

Kathy Whitworth says the big secret about putting is to relax. Other people say that you have to concentrate intensely, which to me means building up tension. I agree with Kathy and think that you should avoid tension. I have a little move that helps me do this and you could develop one of your own, like wiggling a toe or something. That removes the tension and signals that you're ready to start your backswing and sink that putt. Positive thinking helps on the greens as well as off the tees. Putting is one place you can really chop strokes off your score.

Reading greens is another aspect that will come to you with experience. And sometimes experience doesn't help if you run into a different kind of grass. If you play one course long enough, you'll get to know the greens and how they break, where the rises and hollows are so that you'll be reading the greens without even realizing it. You won't have to putt up with (if you'll pardon my pun) what the pros do.

Some women on the tour can just look at a green and tell whether it's fast or slow, which way the ball will break and how hard she will have to hit it for the desired effect. All grass has a pattern of growth, even Bermuda, which is such a tangle it is hard to read. Next to the ocean, the grass will always run toward the water. Anytime it rains, it rains toward the ocean. When you are playing near mountains, remember that the grass always grows away from the mountains. Grass will always run toward any main body of water, be it an ocean, a river or a lake or stream running through the course. There are some courses that are surrounded by water, but there are patterns there, too: The front nine will break basically one way and the back nine the other way.

You want to know which way the grass is going because if you are putting in the direction of growth, or with the grain, as we say, you'll have less friction against your ball so it will roll faster and require less swing. Against the grain, there will be a greater friction and you'll need to put a little more zing behind the ball. Cutting across the grain will introduce a break on your putt, but you must figure out how much of a break. If your ball hits the grain too fast, it might not take the break, but roll past the cup; if you hit the grain slowly, you'll see the ball turn toward home. Unfortunately, there are no laws to the effect that a six-foot putt across the grain will break six inches; you just know it will break.

Even tough Bermuda grass can be read to some extent. Go up to the cup and see which side of the cup the grass is growing over; that will point the direction that the grain is going. Usually, the other side of the cup will be nearly bare because there is no starting point for the grass growth. You'll be able to see whether the grass is coming toward you or away from you, even though you can discern no set pattern from where your ball sits. I learned that from Kathy Whitworth when we were playing in Bangkok, Thailand. I couldn't read a green over there because it was all thick Bermuda grass, thicker than anything we have in this country. Kathy wasn't having any trouble, though, and she was glad to help me. That shows why she's such a great player as well as a great person.

Normally when I putt I don't have to survey it, but I do. I look at it from the side and from the back; from the side to get an idea of how far I have to go and from the back to get the line on the cup. Then I walk up the line to see exactly how the grass is growing along the path that you want the ball to follow (remember JoAnn's tunnel?). From the side, the grass may look entirely different from the way it looks when you walk up alongside that target line. After I've done that, I go behind the ball again and try to put the two other things together in my mind and come up with the right address and swing to sink the putt. The side view, the walk up the line and the view from behind the ball are three check points that work for me. Try them, they might work for you.

Of course, some golfers use their putters as sort of divining rods or plumb bobs or such to get a good line on the ball. Others use the blade of the putter as a compass needle and then take the address position at right angles to that. You have to find your own style.

Sandy's Suggestions Summarized

1. Your stance will be more open with the short irons than with any other club.
2. Practice to find your best address position and the length of your backswing.
3. Don't pass up the practice tee as a place to try some chip shots.
4. Don't try to scoop the ball up; let the club face do the work.
5. With the No. 9 iron, the ball will be back farther in your stance, perhaps at the center line.
6. When hitting out of divots, use a longer club than ordinary and compensate for the direction of the divot by opening or closing the club face.
7. As your game progresses, try using a wedge, a great club for accuracy.
8. In sand, anchor your feet, hit behind the ball and follow through to carry the sand with the ball up on the green.
9. Use the putting style and putter best suited to your tastes.
10. Take time to line up the ball, looking at the line of the putt from the side, the front and the back.
11. Have the back of your left hand and the palm of your right pointing toward the hole.
12. Keep your eyes over the ball and keep your body still when putting.
13. Do not break your wrists while putting but use shoulders, arms and wrists in smooth Y-formation swing.

14. Take the putter back one inch for each foot the ball has to travel.
15. Keep the face of the putter at right angles to your target line.

Chapter NINE

What to Wear, How to Look, How to Act

Aside from clubs, the most important equipment for a golfer is good golf shoes. When you first take up the game, you might not want to go to the expense of buying a proper pair of spikes and can probably get away with tennis shoes or Hush Puppies—just make sure the shoes are flat. When I started playing at eleven, I wore sneakers. I wanted to get a pair of spikes but found that my feet were too small for the available sizes, so I took a pair of my old oxfords to a shoemaker, and had him put on a double sole and spikes. If size is a problem, you can do the same thing.

As your game progresses, you'll probably want to invest in a pair of spikes because they help your game. They are designed just exactly for the way you'll be walking—uphill and down—and your feet won't get as tired as they might in sneakers or regular flat shoes.

When you do decide to pick out a golf shoe, I would advise you to get the advice of your pro again. The heels on the various makes of shoes are cut differently—some high and some low—and if you get a tall heel with a short cut shoe, you are going to be in a world of trouble because your weight will be too far forward. There is no hard and fast rule about types of shoes. A tall woman should not necessarily take a shoe with a tall heel nor a short woman one with a short heel. You can't walk around the course with them before you decide—the same way you can't return high-fashion shoes once they've been worn—but you can let your pro fit them and watch you go through the motions of your swing. There are so many factors involved—you may have flat feet or a short ankle or something like that; you'll just have to try the shoes to see.

Golf shoes are very confining, solid fitting and snug, not like some of the floppy shoes you might be used to wearing. I prefer a shoe that ties and like to have the laces good and tight, although a lot of women on the tour use shoes with buckles.

Naturally, your choice of shoes might be influenced by what section of the country you live in. If you're going to be playing a lot of wet courses, or in the Northwest, Hush Puppies probably wouldn't be too good because they are not waterproof and they wouldn't be too warm. (Isn't there an old saying that if your feet are warm, you are warm all over?) Water-repellent shoes are good for the winter as well as for soggy conditions; they keep your feet both warm and dry. Ben Hogan shoes are weather shoes with a nice cushiony inside. You might investigate these if you have tender feet like mine. I wear a mole skin—sort of a Band-Aid—on my heels most of the year even though my shoes are specially made for me.

I wear Foot-Joy shoes, which cost about $55 a pair. The average pair of spikes will cost from about $20 up. The big difference, of course, is in the fit. I'm making my living in my golf shoes, so I want the best. It's all in what your feet can take; mine can't take very much so I want to be as comfortable as possible. (I think there's another old saying that goes, when your feet hurt, you hurt all over.) If you get a shoe that isn't right for you, you'll have blisters, bone bruises and the general miseries.

Jackie Pung was a darned good golfer who came out of Hawaii in the 1950s. Jackie was a great competitor and a lot of fun, but it took her a while to get used to the way things were done on the Mainland and on the pro tour. She was used to playing in bare feet on those lush courses in Hawaii. Golf shoes were new to her when she put them on for a tournament in Portland, Oregon. At the end of the round, Jackie was so miserable she was about ready to say "Aloha" to the whole tour. Her feet were blistered and in far worse shape than they had ever been, even walking on volcanic rock in Hawaii. She stuck it out, though, for several years and won several big tournaments before giving up the tour in favor of a job as a teaching pro.

The average golf shoe does not hold up too well in the rain. Unless they are Corfam or some other water-repellent material, you'll find that golf shoes tend to get soggy and will need considerable attention. One year, I remember, we were playing in a lot of rain early in the season and some of the women were going through a pair of shoes every two weeks. Now that can run into money, especially if you're not finishing in the money and you don't have a nice friendly manufacturer who is going to keep you supplied. If your shoes do get wet, I'd advise you to stuff them with newspapers as soon as you get home. Let the paper soak up most of the moisture and then put some fresh paper in the shoes. Ordinarily, you should have shoe trees to take care of your golf shoes, as for any good shoe. Your golf shoes might not look like the most important pair in your wardrobe, but they can save your feet and help your game, too.

One thing about waterproof shoes. You might find that they are a little too warm for the summer months. Your feet will tend to perspire because the material keeps the moisture trapped, and you could run into a blister problem. You might want to have two pairs of shoes, or at least switch socks.

Golf socks come in various weights, materials and colors— here's where you can let your fashion consciousness run rampant. They are specially designed to keep from slipping off your heel, with a ball at the top of the heel, or bows in the backs which serve the same purpose. Some women might want to wear tennis socks, which come up over the ankle. So long as they don't slip, these socks are all right, but I don't think that they are as attractive as the regular golf socks.

You might have noticed, if you've played any golf at all, that your left hand takes a little bit of a beating and perhaps you develop blisters there. Playing with a glove, though, is a matter of personal preference. The second time you go out, your hand may have toughened up and by the third time, you might not even notice that there is any extra strain on that left hand, which we tend to use so little in our everyday lives. Some women, and men, too, believe that playing without gloves is the only way to really get a "feel" of the club. If you are one of that group, fine; for myself, I use a leather glove on my left hand.

The glove gives you insulation between the grip of the club and your hand; instead of your fingers feeling the friction, the friction is absorbed by the leather. With the overlapping grip, the glove also comes in handy since the leather helps to hold your overlapped right small finger more firmly. I say leather, because that's what I use; some people use morticians' gloves, which are made of very thin cotton. The women who use them do so because the wetter they get, from the rain or perspiration, the tackier they get. Of course, these gloves are worn on both hands; I don't use a glove on my right hand because I just don't feel right. I might use the morticians' gloves if I had nerve enough to buy them.

I use a special glove in the rain. It's a rubberized material with a sort of sandpaper grip. No matter how wet your grip gets, your left hand won't come off the club if you are wearing these gloves. The tenacity of my rain glove is evidenced by my experience last June. I hadn't won on the tour in 1974 up to then, but I always seem to play well in June—maybe it's a matter of astrology or something, since my birthday is in June. At any rate, we were playing the Medina Open in Ohio and I finished the 54-hole regulation play tied for first at 215 with Gloria Ehret. The last round was played in the rain under miserable conditions, but because of the tie, we had to continue through extra holes.

We played the first three holes with each of us matching par and then had to wait 15 minutes before playing the fourth hole because of torrential rains. It was just impossible to see the ball. We took what shelter we could but Gloria and I, the officials and the few brave spectators who were left got wetter and more miserable. Subconsciously, I must have thought that "this has gone far enough," for on the fourth extra hole, a 321-yarder, I was on in two, 25 feet away from the pin. Gloria was short on her approach and I two-putted for a par while she took a bogey and the second-place check.

A week after that, I took what I considered the big one: The LPGA championship, winning it for the second time. Again the final round was played in the rain. I guess the Medina victory gave me extra confidence because even though the rain was steady when

I teed off, I shot four birdies on the first nine and then held on on the back nine to beat Joanne Carner by two strokes with a 288 for 72 holes.

The moral, obviously, is that playing in the rain can be miserable unless you win. Actually, I don't think too many women would want to play in the rain when they are just out for a friendly game. However, I really enjoy playing in a gentle drizzle—it's great for your hair and for your complexion. If you don't believe me, look at the healthy complexions on those English girls.

If you do play in the rain in a tournament, or are faced with the prospects of playing in the rain, I'd advise you to do what I do—carry rain gear in one of the big pockets of your golf bag. Of course, you should think of this possibility when you are selecting a bag. My bag is big enough so that I always carry an extra sweater with me. It's probably the grubbiest sweater ever seen, and I get teased about it constantly. (Maybe it's like Linus's security blanket.)

The important thing about rain gear is to make sure that it is loose enough so that it doesn't bind or hinder your swing. I prefer something that is practical without being ugly. I can't bear those horrible looking rain suits with the baggy pants and the crotch at about your knees. You look and probably play like a Cape Cod oysterman. Another drawback of the rubberized suits is that they become hot and make you perspire and make noise when you swing. I prefer the tight-fitting but free-moving ski wind suit. I wear a size larger than normal, which fits well over my other clothes and doesn't encumber my swing. My ski suit zips up the front so it's easy to get in and out of without tearing the suit with my spikes.

Wrap-around rain skirts are available for those of you who don't like pants. The most important thing is that you feel comfortable. A lot of times that means you'd feel a lot more comfortable being back in the clubhouse, but on the pro tour, and in tournaments, the show must go on. When it rains, I wear a rain hat—men's style—because it's practical and comfortable. Some ski suits, of course, come with hoods, but I wouldn't want one on mine because it would interfere with my swing.

The contents of golf bag pockets merit some discussion. I think it's a good idea to have a couple of Band-Aids, especially if you are a beginner. Around the seventh or eighth hole, you might be able to ease the misery of a potential blister with the application of a Band-Aid. I also find it's a good idea to carry insect repellent on muggy days.

Some women on the tour carry a little snack in their bags for quick energy. Joann Washam carries peanuts or a candy bar—if it's not too hot—or lemon drops. Shelley Hamlin, one of the newer members of the tour, keeps popping raisins into her mouth during a round as a source of quick energy. Shelley's are supplied gratis by a fruit growers association. You can do whatever you feel is necessary; take a break between nines or use one of the snack bars that most of the clubs now have out on the course.

Unless you belong to a club that has a dress code—and some of them still do—just about anything goes in the way of clothing these days. The old taboos are fading fast and it doesn't matter if your hair is long or your skirts short, just so long as you're comfortable and enjoying yourself. Essentially, it's all a matter of taste and if you are going against trends or trying to be a pioneer, you'll soon know it.

Over the last couple of years, the image of a woman golfer has changed drastically along, I suppose, with the image of women as a whole. When I joined the pro tour, there weren't any stylish clothes. We had to wear long-legged Bermuda shorts and cotton shirts, which always seemed to be pulling out and flapping in the breeze as we took our full swings. Some women were stuck with baggy, scratchy linen dresses. Clothing manufacturers had not caught on to the idea that woman golfers could look stylish and be comfortable. Some clubs were reluctant to change their dress codes, which were throwbacks to the Victorian age. In some places, the club rules not only called for the women to wear skirts on the course, but the rules also specified that the skirts had to extend below the knee.

Nowadays, just about anything but jeans is acceptable. There seems to be an unwritten law that jeans just aren't feminine looking, so the women on the tour avoid any outfit that looks "jeansie." I know a lot of young people disagree with this appraisal, but a lot of young people are not playing golf. Perhaps if we could get more of the "jeans set" on the courses, the outfits would win acceptance.

Three years ago, when we played the U.S. Open at Winged Foot in Mamaroneck, New York, the site of last year's Men's Open, the USGA ruled against hot pants. In fact, the USGA said that skirts could not be more than three inches above the knee. It was a hot week, but we were forced to wear slacks when most secretaries and typists were wearing mini skirts to the office.

In my opinion, hot pants are all right if you have the figure. If your thighs are heavy, you'd be better off leaving the hot pants to the slender gals and passing up the scooter skirts, too. You will be better off in culottes. Now that they are in style, I wear pants often. I even like bell bottoms, not the huge elephant bells, but I like to be fashionable. I don't mind that the bell bottoms flap around my ankles a bit. The women on the pro tour are really clothes fiends; we need a huge variety for all kinds of weather. Part of that comes from the fact that we're more or less in a form of show business, so we always want to look our best. But so do you, and it's a lot easier than in the earlier days.

The big breakthrough in synthetic fabrics has introduced a whole new line of apparel for golfers, as well as for women's wear in general. Regardless of the weather, you can look smart and play comfortably. The new synthetic fabrics are easy to wash—which is important if you are on the move a lot—but there are some precautions you should take in making your selection. For instance, fabric of a warm-weather outfit should have a wide weave so it can breathe; if it can't you're going to feel the heat no matter how short your skirt is or how low your neckline might be.

Cotton is a good material for your warm-weather outfits and I say that not just out of loyalty to Texas. Cotton absorbs moisture and that helps to keep you cool. Although some of the brighter shades of cotton tend to fade in the sun, the whites get whiter. Some synthetic fabrics tend to discolor in sunlight. Naturally, light-colored clothes are cooler than dark ones. I'd also advise you to stay away from leather belts or even leather wrist watch bands in the warm weather.

In cooler weather, I usually wear corduroy pants and a cashmere sweater—not the beat-up emergency sweater I carry in my bag. I prefer things that are soft, that allow you plenty of freedom of movement and don't rub when you twist or turn. There are a lot of materials like that on the market today—Banlon, Dacron, Orlon—to name a few. Bulk knits and high turtleneck sweaters tend to get in your way and interfere with your swing. If it gets really cold, of course, there's always thermal underwear, but it might be too restrictive.

But again, it's all up to you. If there is individuality in your swing, you can be most assured that there will be individuality in your fashion tastes. For your golf game, I've presented options in every case, but the options on picking your clothes are almost limitless. One word of caution: Don't let style override your good sense. Comfort and freedom of movement are of paramount importance; I'm sure you'll find something that will give you these features as well as look good on you.

Some women like to wear hats when they play, but I don't like them. Hats obstruct my vision so I don't wear one, except when it rains. Some women, though, feel that they need a hat to protect either their hair or their faces from the sun and a hat does help in really hot weather. If we're playing in sticky weather, I might wear a terry cloth hat that can be watered down to keep me cool. I don't dunk it in ice water because that would be a shock to my system, but the wet hat is a big help in fighting that fried feeling.

Fortunately, I tan easily so sunburn is not a problem for me as it is with some women. A hat would be helpful for such complexions. Although the sun is healthy, in limited quantities, it can dry out your skin and your hair. Wind adds to the drying process, too.

I wear my hair in a shag cut, with the top and sides short, but the back long. It's a very practical hair-do, I think, because I'm not bothered by long hair blowing in my face and yet I think it's attractive. It sort of frames your face and I think it's both functional and feminine; a lot of the women on the tour wear the same style. If you do have long hair I would advise you to use a hair ribbon which controls your hair without detracting from your femininity.

After you've played a round, you'll undoubtedly want to take a shower or a bath. When you finish, I'd advise a good body lotion to restore the moisture to your skin. Of course, you can do the same with bath oils, but on the tour we don't have the luxury of soaking in a tub too often; it's usually showers, and then we're off in a hurry, but don't forget your deodorant.

I've learned that vitamin E is great for dry skin. Take the capsule, open it and rub it on your face. It's good for scars, too. Just rub the vitamin E on the scars and you'll be surprised at the change you'll notice after a while. It doesn't make the scar disappear completely, but it smooths it out until it's almost unnoticeable.

Playing golf makes it no more difficult to put your best face forward than any other outdoor activity. You know your skin type, and if you need special attention around the eyes, or are sensitive to certain types of cosmetics. There need be no major change in your grooming routine to play golf, just prepare your skin as you would for the outdoors.

Golf etiquette is principally a matter of common sense and common decency. For instance, in your own home, you wouldn't put out a cigarette on your good wall-to-wall carpeting, nor would you do it at someone else's home. However, some unthinking people believe that when they are out on a golf course, they are not bound by rules of property and propriety, so anything goes. This just isn't true; there are rules to follow that will help not only your own enjoyment of the game, but also that of the others on the course.

All divots should be replaced, as I mentioned earlier. Often, though, you will take a divot on the green, or a pitch shot will leave a dent in the green and you will forget about it. That's probably worse than ignoring a divot on the fairway, because the green requires more upkeep and also requires a finer touch. Divots on the green could hurt the next player.

There is a little tool available that looks like a two-toothed comb that can be used to repair the divots on the greens. By putting the prongs under the depression and pushing up, the green is restored. Also around the greens, when you get into a trap, make sure that you rake the trap smooth so that your footprints do not constitute an additional hazard for the players following you.

As a beginner, you will often find that you are slow in taking your shots, and may be losing many balls and making short shots. In such a case, allow faster golfers to play through. Do not tee off until the players ahead of you have taken their second shots. If they are still within the range of your drive on their second shots, it would be discourteous to drive when you might hit them. If you do drive when you think that they are out of your range and you should catch one, or hook or slice so that people are endangered on other fairways, don't forget to holler "Fore." If your ball is a potential danger to another player, give them the courtesy of "fore."

The rules of golf are contained in a 91-page booklet that can be purchased at pro shops on most courses. Joe Dey, the former executive director of the USGA, is probably the greatest living authority on the rules, which date back to 1754. Yet, Joe was quoted one time as having said that "No one is expected to know the rules," meaning that no one is expected to memorize them. Even Joe Dey confessed that he carried a rule book with him at all times to settle disputes or arguments.

Reduced to the basics, the rules state that once you've placed your ball on the tee, you do not touch it again (with certain minor exceptions) until you take it out of the putting cup. The certain minor exceptions covered in the rules include moving your ball from a free lift zone, marking it on the green when you are in the line of another putt, cleaning your ball on the green or if you should land on the wrong green, and moving it off the green, but no closer to the hole you are playing. You will be penalized for touching the ball under any other circumstances.

As a novice, you will probably hit many balls out of bounds. Under the rules, you lose a stroke and distance for such an error. In other words, if you tee off and you think that your ball has gone out of bounds, you can play another ball if you first an-

nounce that you are taking a provisional shot. If you find that your
first ball is, indeed, out of bounds, you can then continue to play
the provisional ball from the fairway. But the first swing you take
at the fairway ball will count as your fourth stroke (one stroke on
the first ball, a stroke penalty for going out of bounds and then the
stroke you took from the tee on the provisional ball account for
the first three shots).

In amateur, or "friendly" matches, this is probably one of the
most ignored rules, either through ignorance or through a refusal
to accept the loss of both the stroke and distance. Many players,
and I'm sure you've seen this, will hit a ball out of bounds and
take a stroke penalty, but then place a new ball down at the spot
where the ball went out of bounds. That is a rules violation.

Water hazards, which add a great deal of challenge to the
game, are of two kinds: lateral hazards, running more or less parallel to the fairway, and direct hazards. If you knock your ball into
a lateral water hazard, you may drop your ball on either side of
the hazard at the point where the ball entered the water, but two
club lengths from the edge. You still must take a stroke penalty,
though. On a direct water hazard, you may drop either behind
the water, or at the place where you played your shot; in any
event, you are penalized one stroke.

If the ball is in shallow water, you can try to hit it out without any penalty, but that is mighty tricky. When I say shallow
water, I mean where at least half of the ball is above the water.
Otherwise I most strongly would urge that you take the penalty
shot. Even when half or more of the ball is exposed, it is just like
hitting a bunker shot; you aren't going to get any accuracy or distance because once that club hits the water the friction nearly
throws the club back at your face. It's similar to hitting concrete;
the club just bounces. If water is covering the ball, forget it; you'll
only waste a stroke and end up taking the penalty anyway.

Very seldom will I hit a ball even if it is above water. I might take my shoes and socks off and stand in the water if the ball is on the bank of a lake or a stream, but even here the conditions have to be just right. Sometimes this approach will bury the ball in a hazard and waste another shot.

"Casual water" refers to natural or man-made (sprinklers) puddles. You are allowed to drop the ball two club lengths from the nearest edge of the "casual water," but not closer to the hole, without penalty. In the pros, we have a similar rule for balls buried in soft spots in the fairways; we may pick up the ball, clean it off and drop it over our shoulder away from the soft spot.

Play the ball as it lies and play the course as you find it; these are two basic rules, but many golf courses will have what they call "winter rules." These "winter rules," which some golfers use in the middle of summer, allow you to lift the ball and clean it and then place it within six inches of its original resting place, but not nearer the hole, without penalty. The idea of the winter rules is to promote fair and pleasant play or to protect the course. When winter rules apply, many people will move the ball before each shot, trying to tee it up, to get that little edge. However, it should be stressed that the USGA does not endorse winter rules, nor does the PGA or the LPGA. Therefore, if you are in a tournament, you must play them as they lie.

Winter rules provide an expression of life-style in golf. If you are going to look for that extra edge in life, you will probably play that way on the course. If you are a straight shooter in life, you'll be the same way on the course and you'll count every last stroke, including the times you whiff. And, of course, that is the only way to keep score: to count each time you hit the ball, all your penalty strokes and the whiffs. It's simple arithmetic, but it throws some people; they have no trouble subtracting strokes, but they can't seem to add very well.

On the LPGA tour, we remember virtually every shot we take; we usually can sit down with the press after a round and describe how we happened to get that birdie on the fourth hole: "I had a good drive, then I hit a No. 3 wood to within twenty feet and got down in two putts." You might think that's a burden to remember, but the pros love to be interviewed.

One of the reasons to count all your strokes is to establish a handicap. The simplest way to do this is to play ten rounds of golf (that's 18 holes to a round, of course) and take the average of your score. If the course you're playing has a par of 72 and you average 80 for the ten rounds (which would be great for a beginner), you would have a handicap of 8. For tournament play, handicapping is a bit more refined. Each course has a rating based on a formula established by the USGA that measures how difficult the course is; there are different ratings for men and women. To figure the rating of your course, take the yardage figures and divide by 180, then add 40.1 to the result. This will give you your course rating for women. The figures are different for men; you divide the yardage by 200 and add 38.25.

In tournament play you use the average for the ten lowest of 20 rounds as a base figure. From this figure, you would subtract the course rating and then multiply that result by 85 percent to get your handicap. Confusing, isn't it? In the pros there are no such things as handicaps, everyone is rated at par and it's a contest between you and your rivals, or, if you like, you and the course, Actually, you need not concern yourself too much with the mathematics of handicaps; if you post your scores the committee that handles such matters at your club will determine your handicap.

If you should decide to take one of those golf cruises or golf safaris before you have established a handicap, don't worry. There are other systems—the Callaway System and the Peoria System—that can serve for the establishment of handicaps on a one-day basis. Under the Callaway System, you are allowed to deduct as many as all of your strokes on your worst eight holes, depending on your overall score and where it falls on the Callaway chart. If you shot 146 or higher, for instance, you just throw out your worst eight holes and the result is your net score. A score of 106 to 110 allows you to throw out your four worst holes. If you shoot a 1-over-par round, you can deduct half the number of strokes on your worst hole. If you match par, you aren't allowed any deductions, but you'll probably have a good chance at the low gross prize.

The Peoria System also discards strokes on certain holes, but it works a bit differently. Six holes are chosen by the committee after all the competitors have teed off. Usually the committee selects three holes on each nine and tries to pick two par-3 holes, two where the par is 4, and two where the par is 5. When the players complete their rounds, each contestant's scores for the six selected holes are added up and the total multiplied by three. From this sum is subtracted the par for the course and 80 percent of the difference is the player's handicap for the round. Thus if you had a total score of 30 for the six holes, you would multiply by three to get 90, then subtract the par for the course, say 72, for a base figure of 18. Taking 80 percent of that would give you a handicap of 14.4, which would be rounded off to 14 strokes.

The handicap line you see on the golf card refers to the degree of difficulty of the holes on the course. The toughest hole would be rated No. 1 and the easiest No. 18. That does not mean, of course, that the toughest hole is the first hole. You might look at your card and see where the No. 1 appears in the handicap line; it could be the fifth, seventh, or any other hole on the course. It is unlikely to be the opening hole since there is no sense getting discouraged right at the start. And that gets us back to positive thinking again: Don't worry about handicaps, course ratings and all those numbers. Just go out and take one shot and one hole at a time.

Concentrate on your grip, your stance, your address and your swing, with your usual rhythm, timing and balance. If you tee off on No. 1 and you see that No. 5 is the toughest hole on the course, don't anticipate trouble. That attitude will ruin your game on the first four holes. Just be natural, enjoy yourself, and play the holes as they come—without anxiety.

Chapter TEN

The LPGA—the Big League of Women's Golf

Golf is big business, with more than 11 million players using 11,000 courses for 15 rounds or more a year. The total of women golfers is estimated at three million, so if you decide to take the plunge and start playing, you will have good company. No one will dispute that the LPGA is the big league of women's golf. We are approximately a $2 million corporation that has extended its operations abroad to Mexico, England and Japan. We grew up financially almost before we knew it, but, unfortunately, we still trail the men in the total value of purses, television time and probably in endorsements and tie-ins, too.

But, we've come a long way, baby, since that day in 1950 when Patty Berg got together with some other women and organized the LPGA. Patty, who still plays occasionally, is one of the greatest goodwill ambassadors we could have; she is constantly visiting charitable and civic organizations in Florida, where she teaches, to give speeches, stage clinics and work with youngsters. Patty, a member of the LPGA Hall of Fame, had 41 victories on the tour.

When Patty and her 11 golfing colleagues got together to form the LPGA, the total purse in many tournaments was $5,000, which is about the average first-place check on the tour today. There were no $100,000 tournaments for women at that time, and a $200,000 event like the Colgate–Dinah Shore Winners Circle was beyond anyone's dreams. The $32,000 winner's check of the Colgate–Dinah Shore would have been a good year's earnings at that time.

I'd like to think that inflation has not been the only factor in the increase of purses; I think that we're catching the imagination of the public and showing that we can play good golf, with all the drama and excitement that attend a men's tournament.

As we've grown, we've naturally attracted many more young women who want to play on the tour, so standards had to be raised. It was once possible to enter the events and play to get an LPGA player's card. That system used to require that the new-comer finish in the top 80 percent of the field three of four weeks, during which time she would be paying $50 a week as sort of an initiation fee. There were weaknesses in that system, though, because a woman could get her player's card and continue indefinitely without ever becoming a member of the association. Since they were not making much money by not finishing in the top 80 percent of the field and weren't helping their scoring averages, we had to put a limit on the number of weeks that they could compete. After that, it was a case of going back home for more practice and then trying again.

In 1973 we set up a qualifying school so that we could weed out the poorer players in Florida before they went on tour. Initially, they had to shoot better than 78 for three rounds in Florida to qualify for the tour and the quest for their player's card. This posed a double standard because they had to qualify in Florida and then still finish within the top 80 percent of the field for three or four events, but they had 12 weeks to do it. The quest for the player's card started when they teed up for their first tournament. In the first qualifying school 16 women tried out and eight made it. The next time, 28 tried out and only three made it.

There were several reasons for the cutback. First of all, we had them on a tough course and then there was heavy pressure to shoot 76 or whatever to qualify for the tour. Consequently, the system was changed so that the candidates had to beat a percentage of the field, which, I think, is a more equitable basis.

Screening of applicants occurs twice a year—in winter and in summer. The screening is important to our image since we want to have only competent golfers on the tour. When we first took applications for the qualifying school, we had 18 to 20 girls who just weren't qualified. The qualifying school is a check on the original assessment made of an applicant and assurance that the LPGA will not be embarrassed by outlandishly poor play by anyone in a tournament. Incidentally, although the newspapers and the magazines might call the new members of our tour rookies, that's a term we avoid—it might be applicable to baseball or football, but we consider our first-year pros talented athletes.

It takes four to six years to become a Class A pro. In the first year, you're regarded as an approved player, in the second year an apprentice player, and then in the third or fourth year you can qualify as a Class B player, provided you've met all the standards along the way. After two more years of meeting standards, you graduate to Class A, where you're expected to play in 60 percent of the tournaments. In 1974 our tour was made up of 30 events,

in three countries besides the United States, so that meant that a
Class A player would be expected to compete in 18 tournaments.
I limited my play, but as head of the tournament committee and
vice president of the LPGA, I kept busy even when I wasn't playing.

Originally the tournament committee was supposed to make
all rulings on the golf course—such as whether the lie was unplay-
able or not, or if an obstruction could be moved without penalty
—but as we've grown, our organization has expanded to the point
where we have not only an executive director, but also two tournament directors who make the on-the-spot rulings. The tournament
committee is still available as an appeals body to adjudicate any
disputes not resolved by the tournament directors.

Since we are in a show business of sorts, some people tend to
regard us as stereotypes—not very bright, perhaps, but talented
in a particular field and with the morals of traveling salesmen. The
"big lie" or the sensational story are difficult to track down and to
refute. People hear one lurid story about an escapade on the pro
tour—and I actually can't remember any sensational ones—and
they think that all pro golfers are that way. It's the same brush
that tars all nurses as promiscuous and all secretaries as just dying to
sit on the boss's lap.

Like many women on the tour, I don't agree with a lot of
things that Women's Lib stands for, but I am grateful that it has
succeeded in demolishing some of the stereotyped notions that
have existed so long about women. The Women's Lib advocates
have helped professional athletes by making people aware that
women would like to have a career. Not because they want to feel
masculine, they want to retain their femininity, but they would just
like to have an opportunity to express themselves in whatever way
they see fit. I agree with Women's Lib in the area of job oppor-

tunities. I know an awful lot of married women are just itching to have their own careers.

Judy Rankin is accompanied on the tour by her husband and her son. I marvel at Judy's ability to take care of a husband and a child and still play good golf—she has been in the top ten in five of the nine events she entered. She is on the executive board of the LPGA and head of the membership committee. It takes a special kind of person to do all that.

Women on the golf tour are just like you and your neighbors. We have the same doubts, the same fears, the same problems. One of my pet peeves is those who say, "It must be nice to travel around the country and just play golf. You follow the sun and have no problems." They don't know that with us it is a job, a business. And like many people in business, there are times when you feel like chucking the whole thing and going home and forgetting about it. That happened to me in 1969. I had been playing for eight years at that time and was tired of it. I didn't feel that I was accomplishing anything in my game. I had reached the point of thinking maybe I should do something else, though I didn't know what. But then I had the knee operation. The rest away from the tour, the time spent at home and the idea of making a comeback gave me a new goal. The rest induced by the surgery was just what I needed and I've enjoyed the game and the tour more ever since.

The prevalent idea that the women's tour is just a lark has its disadvantages, but also some advantages. For instance, many people talk to us while we're playing, although they would never think of doing that with men golfers or with people deeply engrossed in a business deal. We aren't afforded the luxury of saying leave me alone, because we would be criticized if we did. However, the more relaxed atmosphere of an LPGA tournament as compared with a PGA tournament (where the spectators are held behind ropes and not allowed near the players) is a plus. The fairways are not roped off, so the people are close. Our galleries like this, but it could be a problem if 5,000 people tried to come over to you and tell you what a good shot you made.

In the main, we don't do much talking because we're concentrating on the course and the game. If we do have any conversations, it's with our playing partners or our caddies. I've been fortunate in both regards. In the U.S. Open I double-bogeyed the 16th hole and I thought that I had no chance of winning. I was playing with Sandra Spuzich, whom we call "Spooz," and Spooz encouraged me after that dismal 16th. There are only two holes left to birdie, she said, and that's how it turned out. I was on the green with my tee shot on the 17th, but 70 feet from the pin. Still, as I mentioned, I sank the putt and that made me feel better. And then I had another birdie on the 18th. But I often wonder where I'd have finished without Spooz's encouragement.

Another similar incident took place with Kathy Whitworth. I mentioned how she taught me how to read the Bermuda grass greens in Thailand, but there is more to the story. We were playing in the Shell Wide World of Sports tournament when Kathy saw I was having trouble with the greens and tipped me off. As a result, I beat Kathy in the tournament. Naturally, there is no saying whether I would have beaten her had she not given me the tip, but the fact remains that she did and I did. She didn't have to help me out, but Kathy is wonderful that way and helps everyone, including the young players.

The other person I talk to on the course is my caddie. We used to take the caddies at the local courses where we were playing and there were always enough to go around. Then a shortage developed and a rule change allowed us to hire traveling caddies. I have a good one, Nathaniel Jenkins, whom I call Smiley. He's a big help, not only as a cheerleader and source of encouragement, but also because he'll learn all the yardages of the course and tell me exactly how far I'll have to hit each ball. He never gets discouraged. If I don't have a good day, he'll say, "Okay, San, we'll get it. It's not over, we'll get it tomorrow."

Smiley has worked for me long enough to know my moods. When I get out to the course, he'll know if I feel good or not; he knows what kind of a day it's going to be. He knows my game well enough to see if the timing's there and he can cope with those problems. Of course, on the tour, you play regardless of how you feel. We have personal problems just like everyone else, but when you do you block them out; when it comes to doing your job, you cannot let personal problems interfere.

With golf, your mind has to be on the job or you're in trouble, unlike some other jobs. Strangely enough, when you are hurt or sick, the pressure is eased because you have a built-in excuse for not playing well. As a result, you play in a free-wheeling style and do what comes naturally. When you do that, you are going to play better golf. We have a saying on the tour: "Watch out for the sick ones, they're going to play well."

In golf you are pitted against the elements, the course and your opponent. I try to ignore everything but the course; that's where the challenge lies. In match play, of course, there is more of a head-to-head competition with your rival because you play for holes, not strokes. I don't like match play because if I were playing you and I took a 4 on the first hole and you took a 10, I'd be one up on you regardless of the difference in strokes. Stroke play, I believe, is the true test of golf.

While playing, I never think about beating someone, I just think of the course. If you stop thinking about the course and start thinking about your competitor, you are bound to make mistakes.

Along the same lines, I don't want to depend on anyone else for my success. That's why you might play golf when you wouldn't compete in a team sport. Golf is an individual's trial and accomplishment.

Playing in the rain is a nuisance. It's a mental drag as well as a physical hardship. Trying to stay dry and keep your equipment dry is an impossible effort. Hitting the ball is not too difficult if you can keep your equipment dry. The ball reacts differently when struck from wet grass. If you get too much grass and too much water between the club face and the ball, the ball will tend to "squirt" and sail unpredictably. In this situation, I try to hit the ball a little thin, making sure that I make contact with those dimples first. This way I get a straighter, more controlled shot. Those two big victories in the rain should show that I must be doing something right.

Nervous tension is your biggest enemy in golf. If you are tense about playing in the rain you are going to be your own worst enemy. Your mind has to be in control at all times; pretend that it is a dry day and just go about your business. Just make sure that your grips are dry and do not slip. You can experience nerves and make it work for you instead of against you. If you have confidence, you can make your nervousness send a tremendous amount of adrenalin through your system, helping you rise to any emergency. If you are unsure of yourself, you will end up fighting your nerves. Such a situation can even paralyze you; don't let it: Think positively.

Dr. Norman Vincent Peale wrote a book about the power of positive thinking. I'm not a religious person, but I do believe in God and I certainly subscribe to the theory of positive thinking. Actually, I have a thing about St. Christopher, even though I understand that he has been downgraded by the Roman Catholic

Church. St. Christopher is the guardian of athletes and navigators. Since golf is a journey of sorts, setting out from tee to green on each hole, St. Christopher would seem to be right at home on the links. At any rate, I have a St. Christopher's medal that was given me by George Alexander and I always pin it in my bag when I play. I wear another one around my neck. I don't regard this as a superstition, although athletes as a whole are superstitious people. Be that as it may, I only play with white tees—and I have my name printed on them. Now I wouldn't regard this as a superstition unless I got a yellow tee and felt that I couldn't play well with it.

I feel strongly about certain outfits. If I put on an outfit and don't play well in it, that outfit is going to be packed away for a long time before it's worn on the course. I might relent after a while and wear it in a pro-amateur tournament as a trial. If all goes well in the pro-am, I might chance it on the tour again. Another quirk of mine is that I always mark my ball on the green with a coin face up for luck.

I'm not the only one, of course, the other women on the tour have their own superstitions. Shirley Englehorn, for instance, went through a spell where she felt she played well in red. Shirley wore red every day. She must have had a hundred different outfits in red, complete to red hats and red shoes. Pam Barnett went through a similar stage with orange and yellow; she even painted her golf shoes orange, which was really something to see. Pam, incidentally, was the girl who was so excited when she finally broke into the winner's circle she threw her wig high into the air. The spectators must have thought she was losing her head, but she was only flipping her wig.

Men, too, have superstitions. Gary Player, for instance, won't change his clothes or his food when he is leading a tournament.

Paul Runyan, one of the old-time greats, would never change his tie during a tournament. Gene Sarazen—Gentleman Gene, they used to call him—would never arrive for a tournament on a Tuesday. Probably because Tuesday is ladies day at most clubs and Gene didn't want to be caught in all that female traffic.

A lot of this is to be laughed at, and some of us do laugh at ourselves, but continue to do the same things—mark the ball with the coin face up, etc. I think that's important, to be able to laugh at yourself, although not necessarily on the course. That brings to mind an incident at last year's U.S. Open. Sandra Post was playing with Carol Mann, our LPGA president, on the 15th hole when a streaker suddenly appeared. Sandra went into such a laughing fit that she had trouble getting her game under control.

That was the tournament where Carol Mann and Beth Stone were in the clubhouse with 296s when I staged that fast finish for a 295.

Carol Mann is the holder of the 54-hole record along with Ruth Jessen in the LPGA, a score of 200. Carol posted her record in the 1968 Lady Carling Open at Palmetto, Georgia, and Ruth, who also has holed four aces in her career, shot her 200 at the Omaha Junior Chamber of Commerce Open in 1964. Kathy Whitworth, my good friend, holds the record for a 72-hole tournament, a 273 at the 1966 Milwaukee Jaycee Open.

I mention these records because it proves my contention that the LPGA is the big league of women's golf. That's why I'm so proud to have won the LPGA title for the second time in 1974 (I won for the first time in 1965). Winning the U.S. Open for the double was nice, of course, but there you are playing against a lot of amateurs. In the LPGA, you know you are playing against the best because even the women who are limiting their time on the tour turn out for that one.

The Colgate–Dinah Shore is the big one financially and therefore one well worth winning. Not only is there a big purse to consider, but also there is the exposure which can lead to all kinds of endorsements and tie-in deals. The grandest grand slam of all, I suppose, would be to win the Dinah Shore, the U.S. Open, the LPGA and the honor as the LPGA player of the year and the leading money winner. If you won the three tournaments, you would probably take the other two. I was LPGA player of the year in 1970, when I had the highest performance total, and I was the leading money winner in 1966, when I took four tournaments and $40,000.

In the past, money winnings was the way the LPGA ranked its members, but now we have a point system. Under this plan, you get 100 points for winning, 75 for a second-place finish, 60 for a third and so on all the way down to 2 points for a 50th place. This gives us an idea of how our newer players are doing. If golf is a business, though—and $254 million is spent on equipment each year—there will still be credit for the amount of money won. In fact, we are hoping that some day soon one of our players becomes the first to crack the $100,000 barrier for a season's earnings. Kathy Whitworth came close in 1973 and with the purses getting bigger, the chances are improving. JoAnn Carner neared the goal with about $85,000 in 1974.

That $254 million figure I mentioned, incidentally, is just for equipment. Millions more are spent on golf-related items, including glasses, ashtrays, towels, clocks, radios and other items having a golf motif. Look in one of your Christmas catalogs and see how many gifts are slanted toward the golfer. They even have a gadget to keep golf balls warm over night, to get maximum yardage, electrical hand warmers for cold weather, and countless other gimmicks. These are all fine, if they are your particular bag, but for myself, I'll just keep the balls in my bag and keep my hands under my sweater. It's a lot simpler that way and a lot more natural. As I've said all along, I advocate the same thing for you—naturally.

Glossary

 ACE   a hole in one

ADDRESS   the position taken when preparing to hit the ball

AMATEUR   player who receives no money for competition or for teaching

APPROACH   a shot to the green; also, the area in front of the green

APRON   area bordering green, with grass shorter than on fairway but higher than on green

AWAY   ball farthest from hole; player "away" putts first

BEND   a description of a hole not straightaway: it "bends" to left or right

BENT   type of grass used mainly on greens

BACKSPIN   backward rotation caused when hitting the ball to make it hold on green or run back toward hole when landing

BACKSWING   portion of swing from ground to position behind head

BIRDIE   one stroke under par

BITE   same as backspin

BLAST   explosion shot out of sand

BLIND HOLE   where the green cannot be seen from tee

BOGEY   one over par; *double bogey* is two over par

BUNKER   a sand trap

BYE   moving up in a match play tournament without playing, through luck of draw or dropping out of your opponent

CADDIE   person who carries golfer's bag

CARRY   distance ball travels in air from impact point to where it strikes ground

CASUAL WATER   temporary accumulation on course; ball may be lifted without penalty

CHARLEYHORSE   muscle cramp caused by lack of warmup or conditioning

CHIP SHOT   short approach shot of low trajectory

CLOSED CLUB FACE   front part of club points to left (for a right-hander)

CLOSED STANCE   left foot more forward than right in reference to line parallel to target line

CLUB FACE   that portion of the club that comes in contact with the ball

COCKED WRISTS   bend or "break" of wrists as you swing

COMMITTEE   group in charge of tournaments, handicaps, etc.

COURSE   area where play is allowed

COURSE RATING   stroke standard showing difficulty of course

CUP   metal receptacle sunk into green as target for putts

DEUCE   hole made in two strokes

DIMPLE   indentation on golf ball

DIVOT   piece of sod displaced when you take a stroke; should be replaced

DOGLEG   similar to bend, indirect fairway from tee to green, as dogleg to right, dogleg to left

DORMIE   advantage equal to number of holes to be played in match play; a player would be dormie 1 on the 18th tee if he was 1 up

DOWN   number of strokes a golfer trails an opponent; or number of holes in match play

DRIVER   No. 1 wood, straight club for hitting off tee

DUB   to miss a shot or hit the ball poorly

DUFFER   unskilled golfer

EAGLE   two strokes under par for a hole; a double eagle would be three strokes under par

EXPLOSION same as blast; hitting out of trap

FADE shot starting to left and then moving to right at end of flight

FAIRWAY stretch of grass between tee and green

FAT hitting behind ball

FLAG marker indicating location of hole

FOLLOW-THROUGH completion of golf swing after ball has been hit

FORE warning shout to players endangered by your ball

FOUR-BALL MATCH competion where partners combine best scores on each hole; also known as best-ball match

FOURSOME four golfers playing together

FROGHAIR short grass bordering edge of green

GRAIN direction of growth for grass on green

GRASS CUTTER ball that has no height, skims along the ground

GREEN putting surface

GRIP way hands hold club; also, portion of club where hands are applied

GROSS score before handicap is deducted

HALF to tie a hole in match play

HANDICAP number of strokes allowed to be deducted from gross score

HAZARD Ditch, stream, lake or bunker or other obstruction on course

HEAD part of club that strikes ball

HEEL part of club nearest shaft

HOLE unit of play—18 to a round; also, target for putts

HOLE HIGH ball even with hole

HOLE OUT to finish putting

HONOR right to drive or play first, determined by lowest score on previous hole

HOOD covering for golf bag

HOOK shot that goes from right to left (right-handers)

IRON metal-headed club

LAG a putt short of the hole but close enough to be holed out on next putt

LATERAL WATER water hazard paralleling fairway

LEGS tendency of a ball to roll after landing

LINE direction player intends ball to take

LINKS a seaside course (many newspapers use this term for all golf courses)

LIE position of ball on ground; also, scoring references, as, you lie 3 after hitting ball twice

LIP rim of cup

LOFT angle on the face of the club

MARKER object delineating limit where ball can be placed on tee; also, object to indicate ball position on green when ball is cleaned or moved out of line of another player

MARSHAL official keeping crowds back and orderly during tournaments

MATCH PLAY hole by hole competition

MEDAL PLAY stroke play, where total score, not holes, determines winner

MEDALIST low scorer in qualifying round

MIDDLE center part of fairway: "down the middle"

MIDDLE IRONS Nos. 4, 5 and 6 irons

MULLIGAN second ball taken after poor shot; not permitted under rules, which call for penalty for lost balls and out-of-bounds balls

NASSAU competition where points are awarded on basis of best front nine, best back nine and best overall score

NECK place where shaft of club joins head

NET score after deduction of handicap

OBSTRUCTION anything artificial erected on course and hampering swing at ball; local rules cover situations involving obstructions

OPEN tournament where amateurs and professionals compete

OPEN STANCE where left foot drops behind right in reference to target line (right-handers)

OUT OF BOUNDS ground where play is forbidden

OVER strokes over par

OVERCLUBBING using a longer club than necessary for the distance desired

PAR score expected of an expert golfer on a hole or course

PENALTY stroke (or more) added to player's score for rules violation or as specified for lost ball, out of bounds, etc., under rules

PITCH short approach shot with high trajectory

PITCH AND RUN short shot to green where ball travels on ground after landing

PLAY THROUGH   to advance ahead of slower players

PREFERRED LIE   improving ball (see winter rules); not allowed by rules in tournaments, only in noncompetitive play with club's consent

PRESS   to apply more than normal power in effort to overwhelm ball

PRO-AM   competition where a professional plays with amateur partner

PROVISIONAL BALL   ball played and announced as provisional when first ball is thought to be lost or out of bounds

PULL   ball hit to left of target

PUNCH SHOT   ball hit with short, abrupt swing

PUSH   ball hit to right of target

PUTT   short swing taken on green

PUTTER   flat-faced club used for putting on green

REPAIR   part of course being improved, reseeded or the like; usually ball can be dropped out of repair area with no penalty

ROUGH   area bordering fairway where weeds grow and grass is uncut; ball can be played from rough where it lies with no penalty

SAND TRAP   depression filled with sand; same as bunker

SAND WEDGE   heavy-soled club for hitting out of bunker

SCOTCH FOURSOME   team play where partners take turns hitting one ball

SCRATCH   to play at par, no handicap strokes allowed

SHAFT   portion of club between grip and head

SHANK   to hit ball poorly high on heel of club

SKY   to hit ball very high with little distance

SLICE   shot curving to right of target (right-handers)

SNAKE   a long putt with many undulations

SOLE   bottom of clubhead

SPOON   No. 3 wood

SQUARE STANCE   when feet are at right angles to target line

STANCE   position of feet in address

STROKE   score for one shot or swing at ball; total number of strokes on each hole is your score for that hole; also, soft putting movement

STROKE PLAY   medal play; competition where total number of strokes determines winner

STYMIE   when ball of opponent is in player's putting line

SUDDEN DEATH   extra holes played after tie at end of regulation tournament

SWING   overall movement of club from top of backswing to follow-through

TEE   wooden or plastic object to raise ball for drive; also driving area

TOE   end of club; part farthest from shaft

TOP   to hit ball over center, causing it to roll along ground

UNDERCLUB   to use a shorter club than necessary for the distance you want to go

WAGGLE   preliminary movement before hitting ball to loosen wrists

WATER HOLE   hole where water hazard is across or parallel to line of play

WEDGE   auxiliary or specialized club for pitching or for getting out of sand

WHIFF   complete miss of ball; must be counted as stroke

WINTER RULES   local club rules allowing ball to be moved six inches from where it lands to save wear and tear on course (not allowed by USGA rules)

WOOD   club with wooden head

WOODS   trees bordering golf course; can be out of bounds or just rough

Sandra Haynie started playing golf at the age of eleven and has been winning tournaments ever since. In 1974 she won the United States Open and the Ladies Professional Golf Association title and tied for first place in the Colgate–Dinah Shore Winners Circle. Sandra won six of the eight tournaments she entered through September 1974, including the $40,000 Charity Golf Classic in Fort Worth, the $35,000 National Jewish Hospital Open and the $40,000 George Washington Classic. As a result, her earnings rank second only to Kathy Whitworth.